Following Your Path

This *Inner Workbook* is
part of a series that explores
psyche and spirit through writing,
visualization, ritual, and
imagination.

Other books in this series include:

The Adult Children of Divorce Workbook
BY MARY HIRSCHFELD, J.D., PH.D.

The Artist's Way
BY JULIA CAMERON

At a Journal Workshop
BY IRA PROGOFF, PH.D.

The Inner Child Workbook
BY CATHRYN L. TAYLOR, M.A., M.F.C.C.

A Journey Through Your Childhood
BY CHRISTOPHER BIFFLE

The Path of the Everyday Hero
BY LORNA CATFORD, PH.D., AND MICHAEL RAY, PH.D.

Personal Mythology
BY DAVID FEINSTEIN, PH.D., AND STANLEY KRIPPNER, PH.D.

The Possible Human
BY JEAN HOUSTON

The Search for the Beloved
BY JEAN HOUSTON

Smart Love
BY JODY HAYES

Your Mythic Journey
BY SAM KEEN AND ANNE VALLEY-FOX

Following Your Path

Using Myths, Symbols, and Images to Explore Your Inner Life

Alexandra Collins Dickerman

Foreword by Jean Houston

JEREMY P. TARCHER, INC.
Los Angeles

Library of Congress Cataloging-in-Publication Data

Dickerman, Alexandra Collins.
   Following your path : using myths, symbols, and images to explore your inner life/
   Alexandra Collins Dickerman.
      p. cm.
   ISBN 0-87477-687-2 : $14.95
   1. Subconsciousness. 2. Symbolism (Psychology)—Problems, exercises, etc.
   3. Imagery (Psychology)—Problems, exercises, etc.
   I. Title.
   BF315.D48 1992   92-6000
   158'.1—dc20   CIP

Jeremy P. Tarcher, Inc.
5858 Wilshire Blvd., Suite 200
Los Angeles, CA 90036

Type composition and design by Melvin L. Harris

Cover illustration by Lisa Bacchini Graphic Design and Illustration. Copyright © 1992.

For permission to use copyright material, the author makes the following acknowledgments:

Harper and Row, to quote from Mircea Eliade's *Myths, Dreams and Mysteries*. Princeton, Bollingen, to quote from Joseph Campbell's *The Hero with a Thousand Faces*. *The Gnostic Religion* by Hans Jonas, copyright © 1963, by Hans Jonas. Reprinted by permission of Beacon Press. *The Penguin Dictionary of Saints* by Donald Attwater (Penguin Classics, 1965), copyright by Donald Attwater, 1965. *The Gospel According to Thomas*, by A. Guillaumont, et al. Copyright © 1959 by E. J. Brill. Reprinted by permission of Harper and Row Publishers, Inc.

Grateful acknowledgment is also made for permission to use pictures from the Rider-Waite Tarot Deck, which is reproduced by permission of U.S. Games, Inc., Stamford CT 06902, copyright © 1971 by U.S. Games Systems. Further reproduction is prohibited.

Grateful acknowledgment is also made to Grimaud, Paris, for permission to use pictures from the Greater Trumps of the Marseilles Tarot Deck.

The alchemical illustrations are from old alchemical texts. Many of these pictures can be found in Jung's *Psychology and Alchemy*.

If we have infringed upon any copyright material, we offer apologies, and we will give appropriate acknowledgments in all future editions.

Manufactured in the United States of America

10 9 8 7 6 5 4 3 2 1

First Edition

Contents

Acknowledgments

 am grateful for the help and support I received from my husband John, and from my daughters, Lexa and Sarah. I am also grateful to Lori Chaplin, Marian Flanders, Mary McHugh, Doris Dickerman, Tom Dickerman, Tyrell Collins-Conway, and to all the friends and students who took classes and gave me ideas and encouragement.

Foreword

nce in a long while one comes across a book that excites the imagination while it fools one's expectation. Such a book is the one you hold in your hands.

In *Following Your Path*, you are invited to journey into the larger story of your life. You are led with great care and skill to join the personal particulars of your local historical existence to the Personal Universals, with their broadening contexts and more universal formulations. Through a consummate use of imaginal encounter and dialogue with the time-honored structures of myth, symbol, and story, you enter into creative realms of the psyche wherein you find yourself to be the knower, the knowledge, and the known; the player, the playing, and the play. You meet the one and future heroes and heroines with a thousand faces and are astonished to discover that they are all your own. You enter into the archaeology of your psyche, descending through the layered strata of the self to converse with the multiple realms and persona that dwell within you.

In my own research over the course of many years, I have taken depth probings of this layered self and found that our interior world has at least four levels: the sensory, the psychological, the mythic-symbolic, and the spiritual or integral. Each tends to have its own style of imagery and content, logic, happenings, psychologies, physics, and even metaphysics. The psyche is not unlike an archaeological dig in which different civilizations, stories, and interpretations may be revealed at each level.

Unlike the field archaeologist, however, we have living access to the cultures and knowings of the various strata within ourselves and therefore can learn on site how to tap our hidden dimensions for the benefit of our existential lives. It is also possible, with the help of those primordial patterns of meaning and relationship known as archetypes, to build sustaining bridges to, and networks among, these strata, thereby encouraging an ongoing communication and exchange of content— a kind of commerce of the psyche.

In this imaginative and richly innovative book, Alexandra Collins Dickerman has succeeded brilliantly in developing a series of strategies to further that commerce. By having you follow the stages of the classic journey of the hero while deepening the journey with the potent symbols of the Tarot, she gives you access to a universe larger than your aspirations and more complex than most of your dreams. You are awakened into becoming a citizen of this larger archetypal universe. By learning how to live within it and how to abide by its laws and procedures, you discover that archetypal reality is a distinct field of reality, a geopsychic realm requiring a different mode of perception—an imaginative and imaginal mode. The path set forth in this book generates and amplifies the development and greater use of the psyche's capacities. It is the psyche that knows the archetype. The psyche's way of knowing is interior by which it gains knowledge of the images and forms of the archetypal world. You will discover these images and forms rise up as autonomous structures and self-creating works of art with a little encouragement. Those images are so filled with meaning and with patterns of connection and insight that you will wonder how you ever lived without them. And with such productions of the psyche, we discover that it is not psyche that exists in us, but we who exist in psyche.

I have often thought that if schizophrenia—the splitting of the personality—is the disease of the human condition, then polyphrenia—the orchestration of one's multiple selves—would be our expanded health. In *Following Your Path,* you are given profound ways and manifold means of meeting the complex crew that you incorporate. Within you are the Fool and the Empress and the Hermit and the Lover. And within you too are the knowledge and the skills to live and work in an external reality, and an objective world that has become as complex, extravagant, and strange as the one you will meet within your inner spaces. There is little difference between imagination and outer reality. That is why this book will prove to be one of your most valuable tools for preparing you to live and co-create in a time that is, quite possibly, the most critical in human history. I realize that people in other times believed theirs to be the most important time of all. They were wrong. This is it. Use this book.

Jean Houston

Introduction

erhaps you sometimes wonder what matters in your life, why you feel the way you do, or how you can heal old wounds and find the missing pieces of yourself. Maybe you even sometimes wonder who you are.

If you would like to find the answers to your deepest, most intimate and compelling questions, come along. This is the journey that will lead you into the land where your dreams come from, into the depths of your own psyche. This is a journey of redemption through self-discovery, in which you will discover profound insights about yourself. Traveling this way will lead you to personal and spiritual renewal. On this journey you will visit the land of the most vital images of your life. You will find your mother and your father, the demon that haunts you, and visions of your hopes and dreams. You will be able to understand all your most important issues, the ones that have made you who you are. You will find out how you truly feel about these issues, and you will discover what you can do to change whatever it is in your life that needs to be changed.

Your adventure through this book will be a journey to self-awareness in which you will participate in a dialogue between your ego, with its consciously held values, and your unconscious, in whose depths lie a variety of rich archetypal images that reflect the deepest levels of your feelings.

Most of us are unaccustomed to this kind of dialogue with the unconscious. It is a spiritual conversation, and we live in a materialistic culture. Ever since the Age of Enlightenment in the eighteenth century, Western thought has idealized the faculties of reasoning and sensing above all other ways of knowing ourselves. Only analytic and mechanical data have any credibility in our technological world, even though there are other ways of knowing and other scales of values. As a result of the prejudices of our culture, our capacities to imagine, to feel, and to intuit information have not been considered valid ways of understanding life.

However, in this book we will be operating almost entirely on that plane of understanding, by entering into the world of images, symbols, and myths. In this realm the imagination is the central faculty, and we will use it to unite the daylight world of conscious thought with the hidden inner world of the unconscious.

Symbols, images, and myths come from the depths of human experience. They serve the purpose of revealing to us the deepest aspects of reality, which we cannot reach by any other kinds of knowledge. They bring light to the deepest aspects of our being. They uncover our hurts and fears, our wants, desires, and hopes. By looking at myths, symbols, and images, we will actually be able to see ourselves.

Ordinarily, we are only partially aware of the ideas and feelings going on within ourselves, while the rest lies hidden from us in the realms of the unconscious.

But to live whole, full lives we need to be able to understand and to be in harmony with the inner, as well as the outer, world.

Psychoanalyst Carl Jung said that we need to establish the basis for a dialogue with the inner self by using the symbols and images of our unconscious mind, our conscious mind can recognize and respond to. One way to explore the depths of the psyche is by studying our dreams, but they often appear remote and are usually inaccessible for examination without the aid of analysis. But through the use of myths, symbols, and images it is possible to grasp these secrets from within that silently influence our lives. The images in this book will reveal the truths that lie hidden deep in the realms of the psyche.

The exercises that accompany these images are designed to enable you to recognize the voices from inside, so that you can find your way clearly and negotiate successfully through the hazards and alternate routes along your life's path. This book will serve as a guide to the world within, that deep well of the unconscious where, in the words of Jung, absolute knowledge can be found.

Come along and follow your path through this journey of the imagination, where you will discover wonderful treasures hidden within yourself.

The Mythic Journey

This book will take you on a mythic journey involving eight steps. Scholars of mythology have seen these eight basic steps as the principal landmarks that the hero must pass on the journey from innocence to self-awareness. These steps correspond to the Greater Trumps of the Tarot cards, which symbolically depict the sequence of the mythic journey. The following overview of the eight steps will provide you with a sense of direction for your journey.

Step I. Birth
The hero (who is yourself) arises from the unknown. At this stage we already know that in your role as hero you are going to be confronted by adversity; this is the basic assumption of the quest. The fundamentals of this confrontation will become the basis of your journey. This stage is the beginning, a time of openness, vulnerability, and innocence.

Step II. Initiation
Before undertaking your journey, you must be initiated into the role of hero and receive a divine blessing. This is the point at which you must confront the issues you have with regard to your mother and father. You will become initiated as you prove yourself in some way, thereby establishing your own identity separate from your family.

Step III. Withdrawal

Now you must withdraw from the world in order to prepare yourself for later deeds. This withdrawal is a spiritual rite of passage in the rebirth of the self. You withdraw in order to experience the unknown within yourself, which will enable you to emerge later with the divinity you have found there. This step will require the sometimes painful experience of loss of the self in order to find the self.

Step IV. Quest

In a sense, the whole life of the hero is a quest. Every hero in every story represents the search for the self, and all parts of the journey are parts of this search. This specific Quest phase of the search is a time in which you are called upon to prove yourself as you move from the period of contemplation into active pursuit of the tasks of life. This is a time for taking positive action.

Step V. Into the Realms of Death

The hero must face death. This is the time of the symbolic winter, when the world laments its loss and the land becomes barren. However, death always holds the hope that the hero will be resurrected. Thus the death of the hero also holds the promise of new life (just as exploring the dark side can bring forth healing). At this point in the hero's journey to wholeness you move past the physical challenges of the body and back to those of the spirit. You are now called upon to prepare for a voyage into the unknown. This voyage is begun as you enter the realms of death.

Step VI. Confrontation with the Devil

This is the time for facing those things you most fear—the shadowed parts of your life. This is a necessary stage before you can experience a rebirth. It is a rite of passage that will carry you past the monster guardians of the underworld and into the dark night of the soul, which is a vital stage of self-exploration. This is the experience in which you have the opportunity to recognize and retrieve all the various parts of yourself, even your darkest parts, from your very depths, in order to reach wholeness and self-realization.

Step VII. Rebirth

This is the stage of rebirth, a repeat of the experience of the miraculous birth that began your journey. After a violent death, the hero visits the underworld and then returns to life on earth. At this point you have finalized the defeat of death and completed the cycle of nature by being reborn. This stage represents the culmination of the processes of self-realization and individuation, which have created the new you. You have faced and overcome death; you have been able to transform something difficult in your life. The demons have been defeated. Now you can emerge from the depths with new wisdom.

Step VIII. Transformation

This is the conclusion of the journey in which you have learned to connect with the sacred by discovering what dwells inside. You are now ready to be taken out of the cycle of life and be freed of all the old fears and limitations. This is the experience of self-realization that leads to freedom from fear; this is the point where the opposites come into balance in a state of inner harmony. This is the moment when you are able to reach your fullest potential, before you must reenter the cycle of life to begin another journey.

This book is a journal of the experiences of your life in terms of their symbolic content. By the time you have completed this journey, you will have established a language of communication with your unconscious self, and you will have a journal of your progress, as well. Through these pages you will learn the language of the unconscious, so that your outer and inner selves can exist in a state of unity and composure, with each part contributing to the other for a full, rich, and whole existence.

As you journey through this book, you will be participating actively in your own natural process of regeneration, in which the self is in a constant process of growth and self-realization. You will be able to grasp the essential realities of your life and discover new truths about yourself. This journey will enable you to come to terms with old habits, hurts, and fears, and to make changes that will open your life to new depths of meaning.

How to Use This Book

This book differs from most of the other books on the shelf because it is not primarily a book to read and to think about; rather it is a book to experience, as you experienced stories when you were a child, through your imagination, intuition, and feelings.

Each of the following sections begins with a picture and brief description of where you are as you travel symbolically along the eight stages of the hero's mythic journey. These stages are further broken down into twenty-two chapters. Each chapter begins with two Tarot card pictures. The first is from the old Marseilles deck, which has slightly different symbols than you will see on the second card from the more recent Rider-Waite deck. Both Tarot pictures have been included because each presents the same issue in a slightly different way.

Begin your pilgrimage by relaxing your mind and body and gazing at the first Tarot card picture. Some of these pictures may affect you strongly in some way, and you may want to color them with felt pens. Afterward you can look in the color index at the back of the book to find the significance of the colors you chose for the objects in the picture.

Before you begin the Tarot card visualization at the beginning of each chapter, take a minute to relax your conscious mind. This will allow responses to emerge from your unconscious and from the realms of your imagination. Use the relaxation suggestion below, or simply close your eyes and quiet your mind of all distractions and extraneous thoughts for at least a minute or two.

> Close your eyes. Quiet your thoughts, and picture a clear blue sky. In the sky you can see a glorious golden sun, which warms and soothes you as you relax all your muscles and let go of all the tension throughout your body. Your mind is quiet and your body is at peace as you breathe in healing calm, and you breathe out all the stresses and strains from your entire being, and allow yourself to completely, deeply relax.

Following each Tarot card is a brief description of its significance. Next you will find a visualization exercise that invites you to imagine yourself entering into and participating in the world of your journey, which is the land depicted on the card. After you have entered the magical world of your journey, you are asked various questions about what you see, what is happening, why it is happening, and how you feel. These questions will help to illustrate and clarify your experiences as you discover your true self.

Use your impulses and hunches to interpret these questions, and trust your senses and your feelings about what an image means as you let your perceptions gradually evolve. If you should come to an exercise in which no response comes readily to mind, skip over it. A forced answer will be self-conscious and probably have little meaning.

The questions are followed by a box containing information about the significance of the images to which you have just responded, including definitions of the symbols and some ideas to help you interpret your responses in light of their definition. This is the most important and probably the most complicated part of your experience, because this is the point at which you will be uniting the realms of conscious thought with the realms of the unconscious, as you consider the relationship between your response to the image and its significance. The definitions for the symbols in the exercises come from dictionaries of symbols, which are compilations of the cultural, psychological, religious, and traditional meanings of what Carl Jung called Universal Images, and what J. C. Cooper in *An Illustrated Encyclopaedia of Traditional Symbols* calls "an international language transcending the normal limits of communication."

Each chapter includes an affirmation, a short positive message. If you experience an adverse reaction to any exercise (and some include formidable symbols, including the Devil and Death), or if any unpleasant feelings have been triggered, repeat the affirmation to yourself as often as necessary until you feel ready to examine the source of your discomfort. The affirmation will give you a sense of positive grounding as you get your bearings in this strange land.

In many cases several more exercises follow the affirmation. All of these exercises are related to the symbolism of the chapter; most involve symbols from one of the Tarot pictures at the beginning of the chapter. The chapters are also enhanced by stories, myths, fables, fairy tales, poems, quotes, and pictures from diverse sources. These materials present the same idea from different angles, to provide you with the richest possible understanding of the images.

Each chapter concludes with a discussion of the ideas the chapter represents. However, the profound meaning of this book takes place in the realms of your imagination, and its real significance lies in your own experience with the symbols and images. The most important part of this book is the part you write about yourself.

All the chapters will provide you with pieces of information and glimpses of insight. Some chapters will be easy and fun; some will seem trivial. Others will be of immediate, critical importance for you concerning the issues you face in your life today. The chapters and exercises you react to most strongly are those of the most value to you. If you come across a story or an image that affects you strongly, you will know that you have reached a significant personal issue, and you have an opportunity to discover something important about yourself.

Look, too, for patterns or themes in your responses. Whenever you find relationships or similarities in the way you react to different images, consider carefully the meaning of the patterns they represent. When you see a pattern, you will find the theme, the direction, and the meaning of your journey.

The order of the chapters follows the progression of your journey. We suggest that you follow this sequence the first time you go through the book, although you will no doubt find that you spend most of your time on the chapters that evoke the most vivid emotional responses. You may want to embark on this journey again at a later time when your life has changed. When different issues are prevailing, different chapters and exercises will take on new significance, and the symbols will speak to you in new ways.

This book will make it possible for you to uncover your own innate wisdom, which will show you the way to wholeness and fulfillment and transform your life. An abundance of memories, ideas, and thoughts will emerge as you go through these chapters, and you may want to keep a journal (perhaps in a spiral notebook) of the ideas generated.

Proceed along this path knowing that you will discover many treasures on your way and that you will be led safely back again, with a greater understanding of yourself. Take your time and enjoy your journey. Bon voyage!

Step I
Birth

*You have come to the start of a new cycle. This is
your beginning; this is the time of your birth.*

Chapter 1
The Fool

Whatever you can do, or dream you can, begin it.
Boldness has genius, power, and magic in it.

Goethe

 e begin as the Fool, as we walk off the precipice in an act of faith that transcends space and time and all known boundaries. The Fool is unformed, existing in a state of innocence and vulnerability that encompasses all possibilities.

If the fool would persist in his folly, he would become wise.

William Blake

 he Fool is a carefree traveler stepping out into the unknown on a quest for wisdom.

You should begin your own adventure feeling relaxed and comfortable. Look at the picture of the Fool on the previous page for several minutes. Notice the details. Let your mind wander and let your body relax as you gaze at the picture. Now close your eyes again and allow the picture to appear in your mind. Concentrate on it for a few minutes before you open your eyes.

Once you feel you are familiar with the picture, finish the sentences in the exercises that follow as spontaneously as you can. Try not to be logical and self-editing; just let the answers flow as they come to you, accepting them without question. There are no right and wrong answers.

It has been said that images that come from the psyche (or the soul) reflect the psyche. When you allow your responses to the following exercises to arise spontaneously and impulsively from your unconscious, you will be able to view hidden parts of yourself.

It is possible to live the fullest life only when we are in harmony with . . . symbols; wisdom is a return to them. It is a question neither of belief nor knowledge, but of the agreement of our thinking with the primordial images of the unconscious.

Carl Jung

Looking at . . .

The Fool

 magine that you are walking along your path. The day is bright and you feel cheerful, with a sense of openness to the unexpected. You stop to enjoy the view of the mountains below as you make your way up the narrow, winding path.

Around a turn you arrive at a plateau where the grass is green and wildflowers are in bloom. The sky is clear and the bright sun warms your back in the fresh mountain air.

As you walk across the meadow, you see a man with a dog at his heels. The man, who seems to be wandering aimlessly, is dressed in a brightly colored, slightly garish shirt, with a pack slung over his shoulder. A picture of an eagle is sewn on the back of his pack. Although he seems to be precariously near the edge of a precipice, he looks cheerfully unconcerned about where he is going. It looks as if he may walk off the edge of the cliff at any moment, and yet he seems to be completely confident.

As you approach you notice that the Fool is holding a white rose.

Use your imagination and write down the first thing that comes to mind to complete each of the following sentences:

The sun shines behind the Fool, giving him _____
on his journey.

He carries a stick over his shoulder. It is his _____

The Fool is carrying a backpack with a picture of an eagle on it. Inside the pack is

_____

for _____

The dog at his heels is his _____

The Fool is stepping out into the unknown, taking all he will need. His heart is

filled with _____

The Fool says,

I am going to _____

I will try to _____

I can _____

I fear _____

I have _____

The Fool represents you as you embark on a new stage of your life. This figure stands for adventure and openness to new experiences. The sun represents the all-seeing divine force, the center of intuitive understanding. The stick is like a wand, representing the magical powers the Fool will possess on his journey. The backpack is a place where valued and precious things are kept. The picture of an eagle symbolizes release from bondage, strength, and victory. The dog represents companionship, fidelity, and watchfulness.

What do your responses to the exercise of the Fool tell you about your feelings as you begin this adventure? See if you can find a relationship between your response to the image and its definition.

How did you feel about the sun, or divine, intuitive energy? Can you discover anything about your own magical resources from your response to the Fool's stick? What about the pack with the picture of an eagle? Can you find out something about your priorities and values by what you said was in the pack? Was the dog, or faithful companion, a positive image? Do you have good feelings about companions?

Think about your answers and what they mean about you. Remember, any answer that comes from you uniquely reflects yourself. There is no limit to the variety of choices a person could make in filling out the questions in these exercises. Your answers are particularly your own, and they express something important about yourself.

You don't have to have a clear and logical understanding of all your answers. This is not the realm of logic; you will find out as much about yourself from the way you feel about an exercise as from what you think it means.

Say to yourself:
There are unlimited possibilities and opportunities before me. I know I am protected, accepted, and secure as I venture out into the unknown.

Looking at . . .

The White Rose

 magine that you are sitting by a gentle stream on a clear day. The sun is shining brightly. You hold a pure white rose in your hand. When this image comes to your mind's eye, complete the following sentences:

The white rose is very _____

I will put this rose _____

I feel _____ about the rose,

because _____

This white rose reminds me of _____

The sun is _____

and it makes me feel _____

It gives me this message: _____

The white rose represents purity, virtue, and spirituality. The way you feel about the white rose is the way you feel about your own spirituality. The answers you gave regarding the sun indicate your feelings about illumination and perfection. See if you can find a link between what you know about yourself and your responses. How do your answers reflect the way you feel? See if you can find a significance to your responses in terms of your life right now.

Your answers today may be different from your answers tomorrow, depending on your frame of mind. Sometimes your answers will be obvious; at other times they may not seem to make sense until you have thought about them for a while, but they will always provide you with interesting and important information, and often some surprises.

Starting Off

s we begin our journey we will soon discover that, in the words of Mircea Eliade, "A change of perspective can have the effect of a profound regeneration of our intimate being." Seeing something familiar in the unfamiliar form of a myth or a symbol can make it become suddenly meaningful. To illustrate this idea, Eliade quotes an old Jewish story about Rabbi Eisik of Cracow.[1]

> The poor, pious Rabbi Eisik, son of Jekel, had a dream in which he was told to travel to Prague where, under the great bridge leading to the royal castle, he would find a hidden treasure. The dream was repeated three times, so the old rabbi decided to go to Prague. When he arrived, he found the bridge, but it was guarded day and night so Eisik did not dare to dig.
>
> Finally the captain of the guard, who had seen him loitering and heard his story, asked about the dreams and the guard laughed heartily to hear how the poor rabbi had worn out his shoes coming all the way to Prague just because of his dreams. He said to the rabbi that he, too, had had a dream, in which a voice had told him to go to Cracow to look for a great treasure in the house of a rabbi by the name of Eisik, son of Jekel. The treasure was to be found in a dusty corner buried behind the old stove. But the officer said he was an intelligent man, too rational to put his trust in dreams. The rabbi, with a deep bow thanked the guard and rushed back home, where he dug behind the old stove and found a great treasure, which put an end to his poverty.

We shall not cease from exploration, and the end of all our exploring will be to arrive where we started and know the place for the first time.

T. S. Eliot, Four Quartets

"Thus," Eliade quotes Heinrick Zimmer, "the real treasure, that which can put an end to our poverty and all our trials, is never very far. There is no need to seek it in a distant country. It lies buried in the most intimate part of our own house (ourselves) if only we knew how to unearth it.

"And yet, there is this strange and persistent fact that it is only after a pious journey to a distant region, a new land [such as the land of dreams, myths, or symbols] that the meaning of that inner voice guiding us on our search can make itself understood by us. And to this strange and persistent fact is added another, that he who reveals to us the meaning of our mysterious inward pilgrimage must himself be a stranger, of another belief and another race."[2]

God is a circle, the center of which is everywhere and the circumference of which is nowhere.

Hermes Trismegistus

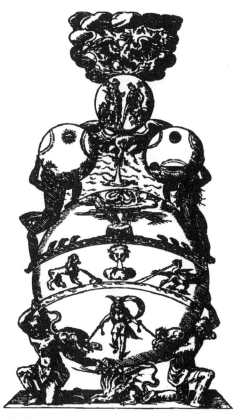

The complex symbolism of this alchemical vase represents the journey of the Fool, who travels from the lower levels of material existence to the divinity of the soul.

Chapter 2
The Magician

The Magician represents the subconscious mind in its humanized form. He symbolizes the ability to harness the energies of nature by transcending the ego.

The magician reminds us of our ability to overcome our lowest instincts and transform them into virtues: our anger can become motivation and energy, and vanity can become self-esteem. All the excesses that corrupt our lives can become modified and turned into blessings. The Magician produces miracles in the face of ignorance and darkness.

THE MAGICIAN

The Magician

s you proceed along your path, you come to a thicket. There are dense overhanging vines, and red roses and white lilies grow all around. You notice a square wooden table standing under a tree. Several curious objects are on the table: a chalice, a sword, a wand, and a coin.

The Magician is standing in front of the table. He seems to be preoccupied, focusing all his attention on what he is doing. In his right hand is a small staff, and he is pointing his left hand toward the earth.

The Magician's table holds the symbols of the elements of life: earth, air, fire, and water.

Red roses grow beside the Magician because _____

White lilies are for _____

The Magician says:

I can be your _____

I will help you _____

I am here to _____

I have the power to _____

I will always _____

Now the Magician turns to you with his wand and says:

The message for you is that_____

The red rose represents earthly passion and fertility. The lily is considered the counterpart of the lotus in the East. It represents purity, beauty, and feminine perfection.

What do your answers reveal about your feelings with regard to passion, purity, and the feminine impulse? For instance, if you felt that the roses grew because of the Magician's power, you may feel that passion engenders power.

The Magician stands for the resources you possess that go beyond your usual physical capabilities. You can find out about the nature of these special faculties from the message the Magician had for you. This is a message about your own magical, or spiritual, gifts.

Say to yourself:
I have a clear understanding of who I am. I am grounded and in control of myself and my life. I use my power to transform my lower impulses into blessings.

Now, think about yourself and who you are. And think about what you want. Close your eyes and find your own center. Connect your center to the earth's center.

Looking at . . .

The Elements

 magine you see an old table hidden among thick vines. On the table are several objects. One is an old coin.

Where did it come from? _____

How do you feel about it? _____

Next to the coin is a wand. Where did it come from? _____

How do you feel about it? _____

There is also an old sword. Where did it come from? _____

How do you feel about it? _____

You also see a chalice. Where did it come from? _____

How do you feel about it? _____

The coin represents the earth. It is the foundation of material life. The wand represents the air. It is the first element, magical power and freedom. The sword is fire, which stands for power. The chalice is water, the source of life.

See if you can find a relationship between each symbol and your response to it. Was one object more compelling than the others? Did you have negative feelings about any of the elements? Did you have any very positive reactions? Think about what you might be able to learn about yourself from your responses.

Guardian of the Spirit

*The Magician goes past the boundaries of the earth
seeking to transcend human nature.*

he Magician represents our ability to possess the gifts and the powers of the spirit. In his role as guardian of the spirit, his capabilities transcend ordinary human nature and the vulnerabilities of the ego. He lives in a world of miracles beyond all logic. He raises one hand toward heaven, where he derives his power. He points his other hand to the earth, where he will use this power. Thus the Magician connects the world of the spirit with the world of nature.

The Magician represents the subconscious mind in its humanized form. He represents the spiritual quest through which he is able to vanquish the internal primitive forces of darkness. For example, the seven deadly sins (anger, avarice, envy, gluttony, pride, lust, and sloth) are forces that can chain us to the ego, to the earth, and to the material world. The Magician represents our ability to turn these forces into advantages by controlling our impulses and balancing them with positive energy. In this way we can be liberated from the downward pull of human nature and transcend our limitations.

The Magician is capable of producing a miracle, an event that goes past logic and overcomes the natural limitations of life.

In different cultures around the world, the shaman or medicine man possesses various amazing powers, such as being able to walk on hot coals and to endure extreme cold. These abilities transcend what we believe to be ordinary human capabilities and yet they are performed by humans who have been trained in mystical traditions.

What meaning can the powers of the Magician have for us? Let us look for the answer, with open minds, in the mysterious depths of life that we have long neglected in our overenthusiasm for the material world.

The Magician is capable of producing a miracle, an event that overcomes the natural limitations of life.

Using Mythology to Discover the Magical Powers of the World Within

he function of myths and the imagination, the qualities of the inner life that can guide us to different kinds of illumination, cannot be proved by observable fact. These are the means through which we can experience personal transformations, which can only occur within ourselves.

Myth is the secret opening through which the inexhaustible energies of the cosmos pour into human cultural manifestation. Religions, philosophies, arts, the social forms of primitive and historic man, prime discoveries in science and technology, the very dreams that blister sleep, boil up from the basic, magic ring of myth.

Joseph Campbell [4]

The images of mythology are common to all mankind. According to Carl Jung, they are instinctive; they come from within us, regardless of what our environment or experiences have been. Myths are composed of universal archetypes, or models. These archetypes are the same everywhere in the world. In different cultures the details differ, depending upon the local geographic, climatic, racial, and other features, but the essential forms and ideas are the same.

Jung investigated and interpreted these universal archetypes in his study of psychology, calling them the archetypes of the collective unconscious. He found that all people use the same images to depict the same experiences and feelings. For example, in nearly every culture throughout time, the tree has represented the joining of heaven and earth.

The object of mythology is to explain the world, to make experience intelligible and to give it meaning. Myth serves as a mirror for our inner life. This is the function and meaning of the mythologies of the world. They reflect the inner experiences of the people who created them.

We can use myths and images to examine and attempt to understand our own lives; we

The mirror was used as a symbol of truth-seeking in the tale of Snow White.

can gaze into the mirror of mythology to find our own inner reflections. Through–out this book, myths (and their domestic counterparts, fairy tales and folklore) are used to illuminate particular aspects of human life on a psychological level. These myths and tales will reveal to our consciousness the activity of the inner self, or the psyche.

When you read these myths and fairy tales, try to understand them in terms of your own emotional experiences. You may, for example, see yourself as Isis (see chapter 3), trying to put together fragments of experience and bits of information to re-create something (Osiris), or to develop an idea or complete a project, as when Isis bore the child Horus.

By looking at ourselves and our lives through the mirror of mythology, we can see things that we are otherwise too close and too attached to recognize. We can evaluate our situations and their context from a detached, almost impersonal point of view when we meet them in the form of a fable or a fairy tale. In this way we may gain a perspective that will give us new insights and answers to real-life questions.

The theme of redemption through love can be seen in the story of the frog prince.

As you come upon a myth or fable, read it and then pause to consider how it might serve as a metaphor to explain a situation or condition of your own life. Examine the myth. What were the obstacles facing the protagonist? Who was the antagonist? How was the task or situation finally resolved? What contribution was the hero able to make after returning from the adventure? Look at the myth for the secrets it may reveal to you about your own situation. What obstacles do you face? Who or what is your enemy? What is the solution? What can you gain and give to others as a result of your experience?

The images of myths are shadows from the depths. Myths can direct our minds and hearts to the mysteries of all existence. Contained within each myth or fairy tale is a metaphor for the experiences in life we all have. Myths can guide us when we become lost or disoriented; they can help us understand ourselves and define which parts of ourselves are in conflict.

An example of a technique similar to this use of myths for self-enlightenment comes from Dahomey, Africa. A person who has a problem visits a sorcerer who will "draw the Fa," or throw date pits to determine which of their gods is prevailing in his situation. Each god is associated with a corresponding myth, which the enquirer examines for its relevance to his own problem. The myth thus gives the seeker a suggestion of guidance. In this way the person is freed of uncertainty and able to make up his mind about how to proceed.[5]

The Journey of the Hero

o understand a myth and to relate to it meaningfully is to rediscover the unknown—the magic in life. You can do this by searching for the intrinsic meaning a myth has for you. You can begin this process by recognizing that the hero's journey is really the journey of your own psyche.

All myths seem to follow a universal pattern or form, with infinite variations according to the time, place, and teller of the tale. In general, myths tell of the path of the hero. The hero goes through an experience of separation from the world and into an experience of initiation, in which he or she assimilates powers at their source. The hero goes off from the ordinary, everyday world into a region of the supernatural, where strange forces are found. In an encounter with the adversary, the hero wins a decisive victory and then returns to the world with the power to bestow on the world the benefits of his or her adventure.

*The path this book will take leading us on the journey inward
is the same path a hero in a myth or folk tale follows.*

19

The hero goes off on the adventure of the soul.

The hero, in essence, leaves the point of origin to embark on an adventure of the soul. The adventure may begin with a battle, abduction, dismemberment, or crucifixion; or the hero might go off into the night sea or into the belly of a whale. At this point, the hero's psyche is fragmented and he feels lost and confused. After various tests, and often with the aid of some magical helpers, the hero emerges victorious: he completes his task, unlocks a secret, finds a missing object, or participates in a sacred marriage. The hero then escapes the underworld or magical forest or enchanted castle and is resurrected or rescued to bring light out of the darkness into the world. In a fairy tale, the triumphs of the hero are domestic. In a myth, the whole society is regenerated and it is the history of the world that is affected.

The hero's journey parallels the nature of all life, the cycle of history and of individual maturity. All things and beings in the world come from an original source. They grow and experience the expression of their power and then flow back into the original state from which they came. In scientific terms, this is the law of conservation of energy. In religious terms, it is the law of God. It is the law of the cosmos and the nature of existence.

The hero is always to be found within ourselves. The adventures of the hero are those of our own psyche as it ventures into the depths to do battle with the subterranean forces and then comes back renewed and victorious.

We experience this adventure on a more mundane level every day, beginning with the waking state, where all reality is factual. Then in a meditative state or in dreams, the essence of reality changes and experience takes on new meanings. This is the level of the unconscious where new answers can be found and new ideas born. Then, once again, the psyche returns to the wide-awake, worldly state. This is the adventure each of us takes every night as we drift off into sleep and into dreams to work out the issues of the psyche, where it is said that divinity is to be found. Then we awaken once again, perhaps to bring our renewed understandings and insights out into the light.

This alchemist picture of the hero's armor shows the symbols of his journey.

Step I in Review

In Step I you, the hero, encountered the Fool and the Magician. Their purpose was to help you evaluate your feelings and assess your situation as you embark upon a new cycle in your life. Write down a brief summary of what you experienced at this beginning point of your quest.

Write down the most important feelings and insights you have gained from your travels through birth, the first stage of your journey.

Step II
Initiation

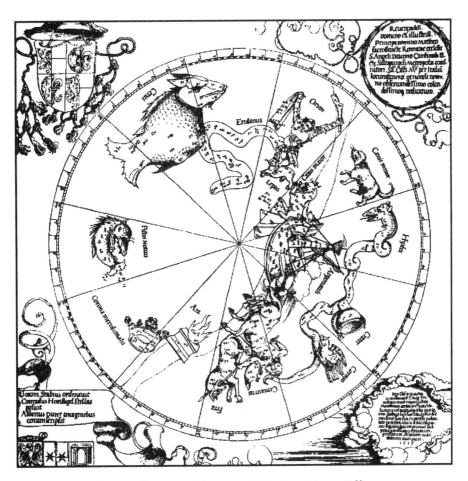

*Now is the time of your initiation. You will soon
meet four sages: the High Priestess, the Empress, the
Emperor, and the Hierophant. They will offer you
the benefits of their wisdom.*

Chapter 3
The High Priestess

he High Priestess is the daughter of the moon. She sits between the black and the white pillars of the active and passive principles, the masculine and feminine states. She holds the book of the divine law in her lap.

THE HIGH PRIESTESS

The High Priestess

 ou have come to the temple of the High Priestess. She sits in a wooded grove holding a book in her lap. She sits before a veil, between a black and a white pillar. You must lift the veil and pass between the two pillars.

The air is cool. Beyond the grove, the wind gently blows through a field of tall corn. Inside, you see the High Priestess, who seems to stare deep into your very soul as you enter her temple. She appears to be both ancient and timeless. She greets you, and at once you feel that you and she have known each other for a very long time.

She tells you that your tasks will be to learn to distinguish the real from the false, to hear the sound that is silent, and to see the invisible. The High Priestess says to you, "Within yourself is the key and therein all mysteries will unfold."

The land of the psyche lies beyond the two pillars,
where we can reach transcendence.

The High Priestess says:

I am here for _____

I can always _____

I remember your _____

I know that you _____

I will _____

She will give you the knowledge of _____

She will remind you that _____

The High Priestess says to you:

Harmony, balance, and integration will come through _____

_____

_____

_____

_____

The symbol of the High Priestess represents the subconscious mind in its pure state. It is yin—the yielding, gentle, receptive, tolerant, merciful, and withdrawn state of mind. The subconscious mind can take scattered fragments of ideas and form them into new ideas ready to be reborn as insights and inspirations.

Your responses to the exercise of the High Priestess will provide you with knowledge from within yourself.

The High Priestess represents the subconscious mind in its pure state.

Say to yourself:
All knowledge and understanding are within my reach
when I look within myself.

Looking at . . .

The Message

The High Priestess has a message for you. She wants you to know that _____

_____

She has a gift for you. It is _____

This is a message to you from your subconscious mind and an indication of
the nature of your own innate gifts.

How do you feel about these gifts? _____

_____

What are you going to do with them? _____

_____

Looking at . . .

The Two Pillars

The High Priestess suggests that you look more closely at the two pillars at the entrance to her grove. One pillar is black, the other white.

There is a message for you on the black pillar. It says: _____

_____

There is a message on the white pillar. It says: _____

_____

You walk between the two pillars. You feel _____

_____

When you have passed through the pillars, you find _____

_____

The two pillars represent the dual aspect of life. The black pillar is the feminine and unconscious side; the white pillar represents the masculine, material world. Walking between the pillars represents entering into the world of the psyche.

This exercise will give you some insights about your feelings concerning these two sides of yourself. It will tell how you feel about entering into a new level of self-awareness. What you find on the other side of the pillars is a metaphor for what you will find in your subconscious.

Looking at . . .

The Scroll

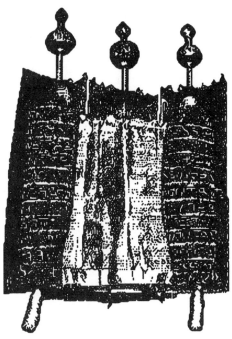

Imagine you have come upon an ancient scroll in the temple of the High Priestess. On it there is a message for you. Close your eyes and read the message.

It says: _____

_____

_____

_____

> The scroll represents the Book of Life. This exercise will give you some idea of what your own book of life holds at this point along your journey.

The symbol of the High Priestess can be described in terms of the following myth of Isis and Osiris.

The Myth of Isis and Osiris

 hen Osiris came to the throne as pharaoh of Egypt, the Egyptians were very warlike. This was soon altered when he and the queen, his sister Isis, came into power. After they had taught the arts of peace and civilization to the people of the land from the Delta and upper Egypt as far as Thebes, Osiris left his younger brother, Set, to rule, and went off to civilize the people of more distant lands.

When he left, Osiris took no army. He took only a band of priests and musicians. Wherever he went, most of the barbarians of even the wildest tribes were won over by his wise words and sweet music. But not all the people followed Osiris. Evil was awake in the world, striving against good. The leader of evil was Set.

As soon as Osiris returned home, Set prepared him a feast of honor. Osiris, suspecting nothing, came unattended. After the meal, Set had a beautiful cedarwood chest inlaid with precious jewels brought into the banquet hall. Set said, "Here is my gift to one of the guests. It shall belong to whomever it fits."

All the guests tried to fit into the chest, but it was too tall or too short, too fat or too thin for each of them. Then Osiris climbed into the chest and it fit him perfectly. Osiris cried out, "The chest is mine! It fits as if it were made for me!"

Isis, Egyptian mother goddess

"It is indeed yours," cried Set. "It is the chest in which you shall die." He slammed down the lid and had it nailed shut and sealed with molten lead. Then he threw it into the Nile.

As the chest floated in the river, a great wave hurled it into a tamarisk tree. The tree quickly clasped its branches around the chest until it was completely hidden within its trunk.

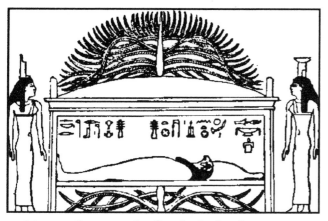

Osiris was shut up in the chest by his brother.

After many years of searching, Isis finally found the tree that housed the chest. The rulers of that land, Queen Astarte and King Malcander, agreed to give Isis a favor in return for her blessings, and Isis asked them for the tamarisk tree. When it was given to her, Isis set the coffin on a boat and sailed off. Finally she reached an island, where she hid the chest in the reeds of the Delta until she could perform the funeral rites.

Set discovered the chest. Enraged, he snatched out the body of his murdered brother and tore it into seven pieces, which he scattered throughout the land of Egypt. "Now I have destroyed Osiris and kept his spirit out of the afterworld," he cried.

When Set was gone, Isis crept out of her hiding place and went in search of the pieces of her husband's body. Her distress was so great as she rode up and down the Nile, even the crocodiles pitied her and let her pass.

With the aid of Anubis, the son of Set and Nepthys, who took the shape of a wild dog to help the search, Isis was able to find all but one

Isis and Anubis (who took the shape of a wild dog) found the pieces to put Osiris together again.

piece of the body. Isis performed a magic ritual to put Osiris' body together again and bring him back to life.

Later she and Osiris had a son, whom they named Horus.

When Osiris finally died, his spirit passed into the Duat, where he became King of the Dead, welcoming all those who were found worthy to enter his kingdom and adding them to his army of the blessed with whom he would return to reign on earth after the last great battle with Set.

Once the pieces of Osiris were found, Isis performed a magic ritual that reconstructed and reanimated him.

Osiris represents our immortal, divine side, which cannot be destroyed or vanquished; it can come up out of the coffin of molten lead and survive fragmentation and mutilation.

Consider your own life in terms of the complex symbolism of this myth. Have you felt persecuted by warlike impulses? Are you collecting fragments of ideas and information to put them together in the form of a new idea? Or are the parts of yourself and your life so fragmented and scattered that nothing adds up and makes sense? The myth of Isis tells us we can always go back and collect the pieces, put them together, and go on to create something new and wonderful.

Looking at . . .

The Box

magine you are inside a box. What does the box look like?

_____

What is it made of? _____

What color is it? _____

Describe the box. _____

How do you feel about being inside this box? _____

_____

Can you get out? How?_____

Do you want to get out? _____

Will you get out? When? Why? _____

_____

The box is the symbol of the material body (containing the unconscious). It will often give you a sense of your present frame of mind.

What is your box made of? Is it threatening to you or is it comfortable? Look up the symbolism for the color of your box in the color index at the back of the book.

How did you feel in the box? What does this indicate about the way you are feeling about your life? Did you feel confined in your box? Could you get out? (If not, close your eyes and imagine a way to get out. You could open up a door or build some stairs.)

Looking at . . .   *Your Seven Parts*

Imagine there are seven parts of yourself. What would they be?

List the parts and what they look like:

1. _____

_____

2. _____

_____

3. _____

_____

4. _____

_____

5. _____

_____

6. _____

_____

7. _____

_____

If one part were missing, which one would it be? _____

Where could you find it? _____

We are comprised of many different aspects and sometimes, like Osiris, we may become scattered. This exercise will help you to clarify your sense of who you are and how to integrate the different facets of yourself.

Looking at . . .

The Facilitator

This is an exercise to help you develop the powers of your inner mind to solve problems and gain insights to fit all the fragments of your ideas and experiences together.

Write down a problem or situation that has been bothering you. Imagine there is a person or a mythical being who is able to give you the perfect solution to the problem or situation.

What is the name of this being? _____

What does he or she look like? _____

What is he or she wearing? _____

Describe this being as fully as you can. _____

_____

_____

Now ask for the solution to your problem. What is the solution? _____

_____

What advice does the facilitator offer concerning the best way for you to proceed?

_____

The angel with a wreath is a symbol of victory.

Whenever you face a difficult dilemma, use the image of the facilitator to find answers and discover solutions.

Another aspect of the symbolism of the High Priestess may be seen in the following folktale.

The Story of the Hedley Kow

nce upon a time there was an old woman who lived on the edge of a forest. She earned her living by doing errands and odd jobs for the nearby farmers and villagers. She usually had only enough money to buy some bread and cheese for her supper, but she was a cheerful soul, without a care in the world. Every day she would get up early to gather pine cones and branches for her evening fire. Then she would set out to look for work. Her cottage was poor and old, but the old woman didn't mind; she was contented with her life.

The farmers' wives made sure the old woman was on her way home long before dark, because after nightfall the Hedley Kow, a hobgoblin, was known to haunt the roads. All the villagers were afraid of him. He could change his shape and frighten people out of their wits. He liked to chase them home and trick them with mean pranks.

One summer evening as dusk approached, the old woman was still on the road hastening toward home. On the side of the road she saw a big black pot. She wondered who would leave such a fine pot on the road, so she went over to examine it. "Maybe it has a hole in it and someone threw it out, but I could find a use for it myself," she said as she looked inside.

"Oh glory!" she exclaimed when she peered into the pot. "It is filled with gold coins!" For a while she just stood and gazed at her find, admiring the sparkle and shine of her treasure. "What a lucky person I am," she said to herself, and she pulled at the pot to see how heavy it was. She decided the only way she could manage to get such a heavy load home was to tie one end of her shawl to it and drag it along the road. "I can think about what to do with my fortune all night long as I drag it home," the old woman mused, as she pulled and tugged the pot along.

"I could buy a grand new house or I could keep some gold coins on the mantle by the fireplace. I could bury the treasure at the foot of the garden." By this time, the old woman was growing tired from dragging the pot, so she stopped to take a rest.

When she peeked into the pot to look at her treasure, she found no gold. In its place was a shining lump of silver. In disbelief she checked the pot again, but there was still a great lump of silver inside.

The old woman dragged the heavy pot down the road.

"I could have sworn there was gold in this pot when I found it, but I must have been dreaming," the old woman thought. "Well, maybe this is better anyway. Gold pieces are hard to keep safe. This will be easier to keep and I am still a rich woman. Oh, but I am the lucky one!" So the old woman continued her trudge homeward, cheerfully thinking of all the things she could do with her fine lump of silver.

Before long she again tired from dragging the heavy pot, so the old woman stopped to rest.

Once again, she checked inside the pot to look at her treasure. This time she was astonished to find that the silver was gone and in its place was a lump of lead.

"Mercy me!" the old woman exclaimed. After a moment's thought, she said to herself, "Well, this is a convenient turn of luck. I will have no trouble selling this lead, and I will have a lot of pennies for it! Now I won't have to stay awake nights worrying about being robbed of my gold or silver."

The old woman continued her slow journey along the road, dragging the pot behind her and chuckling over her good luck. Soon she stopped to rest again. This time when she checked the pot, she found that the lump of lead had vanished and in its place was a large stone. "My, my," the old woman exclaimed. After a moment she said to herself, "This is indeed a piece of luck! This is just the size stone I have been looking for to keep my door open while I bring in the wood for my fire. I am a lucky woman!"

So she dragged her pot down the road, thinking about how well her stone would work as a doorstop. When she finally reached her cottage, she bent her stiff back to pick up the stone, when all of a sudden the stone gave a squeal! Arms and legs and large ears appeared as a creature emerged, laughing and pointing his finger, making ugly faces at her as he danced around the small room.

The old woman stared at the creature in amazement. "Well, well," she exclaimed. "If I'm not the luckiest old woman! Imagine, the Hedley Kow in my own house!"

The Hedley Kow emerged from the pot, pointing his finger and making ugly faces at the old woman.

The little man stopped short. "Do you mean to tell me that you are not afraid of the Hedley Kow?" he asked.

"Oh no, I am not afraid of you," the old woman replied. "You are a rare sight to see, and besides, you have done me no harm." She wrapped her shawl around her shoulders and nodded her head. "Good evening to you," she said, and she went to the fireplace to fix her tea.

The little man turned around dejectedly, scratching his white beard as he walked out the door. "Now," the old woman called to him as he left, "I don't have much, but you are welcome to share some bread and cheese and a cup of good hot tea, if you would like to join me for supper."

As the two sat down to eat, the little bit of cheese became a fine large block, and fresh fruit and a loaf of sweet brown bread appeared. The two shared a cheerful meal. After they had eaten their fill, they sat comfortably by the fire. The Hedley Kow entertained the old woman with stories of his pranks and adventures until tears ran down her cheeks. "I have never had such a fine evening as this has been," she said.

After that, the Hedley Kow came to join the old woman for supper and to visit quite often. And the old woman found that her woodpile was always full and her cupboard was never empty. Wisely, she said nothing to her neighbors about her new friend. When the village folk cursed the Hedley Kow for his mischief, the old woman would merely say, "Oh, he isn't so bad, he just likes to stir up some mischief from time to time."

In this story, the old woman was not afraid of the hidden parts of her psyche, or her unconscious self, which is represented by the contents of the pot and the hobgoblin. Instead, she was trustful and welcoming of whatever should appear, not judging its apparent material worth but accepting it on its own merits. As a result, all of her needs were met and she was happy and contented, living in harmony between the inner and the outer worlds, the black and the white pillars of the High Priestess—or in this case, the Hedley Kow and the village folk.

Reflections . . .

The Realms of the Unconscious

The symbolism of the High Priestess reveals to us that by examining our lives in terms of our inward needs, we can take into account the symbolic dimensions of our minds.

Now that neurophysiologists have discovered that the right hemisphere of the human brain is predisposed to thinking in intuitive, spontaneous, and sensory terms, we have become more able to accept that type of process as authentic. Once we have established that half of the brain thinks in metaphors and symbols, we are free to acknowledge the existence of that world where poetry, music, art, and feelings are more important than money and machinery.

In following chapters we will explore various methods of tapping the processes of the right hemisphere. We can reach beyond our limitations into dimensions that connect us with the cosmos, that essence of life the Eastern mystics and the Western spiritualists have always known about, where the cosmic and the human become one.

In the past, myths played the part that counselors, therapists, and psychologists or psychiatrists do today in helping us understand who we are and how to live our lives. We will be able to achieve a sense of meaning and wholeness when we learn to unite the two sides of the brain in a harmonious balance.

The role of psychology is to serve modern man until there is some new point of view that will help us find believable and liveable meaning in our lives, which have lost a sense of meaningfulness.

Otto Rank

The High Priestess represents the long dormant processes of the creative, idealistic, poetic part of the self. This is the domain of the artist and the poet, and this is the side we have neglected. Yet these are the attributes that can lead us to the discovery of a sense of purpose and fulfillment. The message of the High Priestess is that we need to rediscover our ability to dream and to feel. The two pillars are the doorway to the psyche, whose language is not made of words. It speaks through the medium of images, metaphors, and dreams. In order to listen to our inner wisdom, we must discover and understand these images; these are the images that are loaded with significance. This is the meaning that brings us direction, satisfaction, and fulfillment.

Alfred Adler said that we know more than we understand. Our powers to think and analyze lag far behind our intuitive powers. When we learn to trust our intuitive images, they will guide us safely through the trials of life.

*Beyond the two pillars, which represent the paired opposites in
life, is the land of the psyche, where we can find balance
and ascend the ladder, transcending the
limitations of ordinary life.*

Chapter 4
The Empress

 he Empress is the mother goddess, the mother of mental images. In Greek mythology she is Demeter, the source of ideas and images from the springs of the unconscious mind. It was she who gave humankind the gift of wheat. She showed us how to plant the seed, cultivate, and finally harvest the wheat and grind it. She represents mother nature, with whom we must come to terms. We have come into her domain, where she can teach us many things if we have the wisdom to listen to her.

Looking at . . .

The Empress

n a field of fragrant violets, lilies, ivy, lilacs, wheat, and blossoming pomegranate trees, grasses ripple and birds sing. The beehives are alive with springtime; the trees whisper and the river murmurs in the living joy of nature.

The Empress sits on her flowering throne with a crown of greenery on her head. Behind her are two snow-white wings. She holds a scepter in her hand. She says to you, "I send you along the stream past the flowers and the wheat fields, through the forest of many trees, in search of _____

_____

which you will find in the _____

_____

I am clothed by the sun, and the moon is beneath my feet. I am your _____

_____

I can _____

I will give you _____

I have _____ for you.

Now the Empress smiles and opens her arms to you.

She says to you, _____

_____

_____

_____

The mother goddess represents nature and the instinctive part of your psyche. She is the mother of your intuition and creative imagination. What guidance and inspiration does she have for you?

The Anima Mundi, or world mother

Say to yourself:
I have a blossoming garden of creative potential that is nurtured
to fruition for my highest personal fulfillment.

Looking at . . .

The Ancient Altar

This exercise is useful whenever you are troubled by events beyond your control. It can also help you overcome stress by helping you let go of your anxieties and emotional burdens.

lose your eyes and relax your body and your mind. Imagine you are standing in front of a fire that is burning at an ancient altar. See yourself pick up several leaves from the ground. On each leaf is the name of something that has been bothering you. Write down the names of the leaves: _____

_____   _____

_____   _____

_____   _____

_____   _____

_____   _____

_____   _____

_____   _____

Take the leaves, one by one, and throw them into the fire. Watch as each leaf burns and turns to smoke. Watch the smoke rise and float off into the sky, taking your problems with it.

How do you feel? _____

_____

Looking at . . .

The Locket

Imagine you have come across a heart-shaped locket.

What is it made of? _____

What is inside? _____

How do you feel about the locket? _____

What will you do with it? _____

Write in the name that belongs in the center of the heart: _____

The heart represents the wisdom of feeling, of following one's heart rather than the wisdom of rational knowing. The heart represents compassion, understanding, love, and charity.

 Is your heart made of something valuable? The things inside represent the feelings you treasure.

The Myth of Cybele, the Great Mother

 t is told that the Great Mother Goddess was born in Phrygia. In ancient times, Meion became king of Phrygia and Lydia. He married Dindyme, who gave birth to a daughter. Furious at having a daughter instead of a son, the king abandoned the infant to be exposed to the elements and perish on Mount Cybelus.

The ferocious beasts kept Cybele safe from harm.

However, leopards and other ferocious beasts found the infant and protected her. The shepherd women who tended their flocks on the mountain were astonished to find the baby girl who was tended by the beasts. They called her Cybele, after the mountain.

The child grew to be strong and beautiful, and she came to be admired for her intelligence. She was the first to devise the pipe of many reeds, and it was she who invented the cymbals and the kettledrums that accompany games and dances. In addition, she taught the people how to use rites of purification to heal sickness of both the flocks and of children.

Cybele saved babies from death by her spells. Her devotion and her love led all the people to revere her and call her the Mother of the Mountain.

The Song of the Goddess

am she that is the natural mother of all things, mistress and governeses of all the elements, the initial progeny of worlds, chief of the powers divine, queen of all that are in hell, the principal of them that dwell in heaven, manifested alone and under one form in all the gods and goddesses. At my will the planets of the sky, the wholesome winds of the seas, and the lamentable silences of hell be disposed; my name, my divinity is adored throughout the world, in divers manners, in variable customs, and by many names. For the Phrygians that are the first of all men call me the Mother of the gods of Pessinus; the Athenians, which are sprung from their own soil, Cecropian Minerva; the Cyprians, which are girt about by the sea, Paphian Venus; the Cretans, which bear arrows, Dictynian Diana; the Sicilians, which speak three tongues, infernal Proserpine; the Eleusians, their ancient goddess Ceres; some Juno, others Bellona; others Hecate; others Rhamnusia, and principally both sorts of the Ethiopians, which dwell in the Orient and are enlightened by the morning rays of the sun, and the Egyptians, which are excellent in all kinds of ancient doctrine, and by their proper ceremonies accustomed to worship me, do call me by my true name, Queen Isis. Behold I am come to take pity on thy fortune and tribulation.

Apuleius, *The Golden Ass*

The goddess depicted as the mother and queen of all things.

The Myth of the Mother Goddess

emeter, the great mother goddess, had a daughter named Persephone, the maiden of spring. One day Persephone strayed too far when she was picking flowers in a meadow with her companions. The lord of the dark underworld, the king of the dead, carried her away in his chariot.

When Demeter learned of the abduction of her beloved daughter, she searched all over the land for her. Finally, she learned that Persephone was under the earth, among the shadowy dead.

Demeter mourned for her lost daughter. In her great sorrow she withdrew her powers from all the crops, and the earth became barren. Nothing grew; no seed sprang up and winter covered the earth. The goddess refused to let the earth bear fruit until she had seen her daughter.

After many complaints from the gods, Zeus sent his messenger into the underworld to get Persephone back. But the lord of the underworld had persuaded Persephone to eat a pomegranate seed, knowing that if she did she must return to him.

Demeter was filled with joy at the return of her daughter, and she made the fields rich with abundant harvests. But for six months every year, Demeter loses her daughter to the lord of the underworld. And during this time the world is barren, as the goddess mourns.

Demeter, with sheaves of wheat, pomegranates, and a beehive.

Reflections . . .

Messages from the Underworld of the Mind

ithout the emergence of ideas that come up from the subconscious, we are left to a barren winter of our own despair. In the inevitable cycle of life, there are times when we feel abandoned. We grieve until the return of the lost parts of ourselves from the underworld, or the inner mind, whereupon we become revitalized. We can then once again rediscover the sources of our joy and inspiration, and life is born anew.

The unconscious is the underworld, the source of our images. Without them, life is bleak and barren, but the uninspired time of our winter is a necessary period of struggle before the reawakening, the springtime of new ideas.

The world in which we live is filled with stimulation. We are constantly being bombarded by sound, color, and action. Even in our inactive moments we provide ourselves with the stimuli of TV, radio, records, and movies, as well as incessant internal chatter. Seldom do we shut out this outer world to listen to the world inside.

It is possible and important for us to learn to quiet the noise and constant demands of the external world. Meditation, for example, is an ancient method for concentration on the quiet within. When we learn to silence the outside noise, we can discover the richness deep inside.

When the external world has been quieted, we can turn to the art of visualization. Visualizing can have remarkable power over many aspects of our lives. Visualizing mental pictures has been shown to be at least as significant as any outer form of experience. A classic example of this is a widely quoted experiment (from *Research Quarterly* by Alan Richardson) on the effects of mental practice on improving skills for sinking basketballs.

A test group of students practiced shooting baskets every day for twenty days, and were scored on the first and last days. A second group was scored on the first and last days, but they engaged in no basketball practice during the twenty test days. A third group was scored on the first day. Then for the twenty test days, they spent twenty minutes a day *imagining* they were shooting baskets. If they missed, they would readjust their aim and try again (in their imagination only). The first group, which had actually practiced, scored an improvement of 24 percent. The second group, with no practice, showed no improvement. The third group, which had practiced in their imagination only, scored an improvement of 23 percent! This illustrates that mental pictures and mental exercise can be as powerful and effective as actual physical experience itself.

Physiologists who have studied the brain have discovered that actual physical change occurs when a person sitting in a laboratory visualizes a frightening object. Likewise, when a person imagines something soothing, the body responds; the heart rate lowers, blood pressure decreases, and muscles relax.

Visualizing

t is easy to learn the techniques of visualization by learning to focus the mind on an imagined object. As we visualize something, we begin to identify with it just as if it had been an actual experience. Thus we can visualize a desired goal (as the basketball shooters did) and actually mentally become part of the picture. For example, if you feel anxious about a lecture you are to give, you can visualize yourself delivering a brilliant talk. Once you have visualized yourself performing effectively, the experience becomes part of your background, a successful history on which to draw for future use. When you give the actual talk, the experience feels familiar and is much less threatening because you have the confidence of having already performed the task successfully.

Imagery and visualization techniques have been used throughout history as effective tools for healing. Visualization is used by shamans to create harmony in the sick person and reunite him with his soul. The technique was used in Hermetic philosophy to cure disease by visualizing perfect health. The ancient Greeks had their patients dream of being healed by the gods.

Relaxation and visualization are gaining respect as methods for treating disease today. We have begun to discover broad uses of visualization and imagery for all aspects of life, whether to heal sickness or simply to enrich the quality of our everyday experiences and to increase our ability to understand our lives. Through visualization we can reach past the barriers that separate us from the deepest parts of ourselves, to open up sources of power and healing that will take us beyond the limits of the material world.

This is the message of the Empress.

*The Empress is the mother of ideas and images
from the unconscious.*

Chapter 5
The Emperor

he Emperor represents the masculine, paternalistic aspect of the psyche, the father who rules the world from his throne. On his head he wears a crown, symbol of his dominion. He represents the powers of reason, regulation, and order. The Emperor upholds the status quo. He is a practical and powerful administrator of the material world who regulates life by his law.

Looking at . . .

The Emperor

 ou have entered the land of the empire. The Emperor's castle lies past the long road and across a deep moat. You have been given a password that will allow you to travel safely into the realms of the Emperor. To visit the castle you must travel past the guards until you reach the castle itself. Here you are escorted into the Emperor's audience chamber.

The Emperor is sitting on his throne beside a huge blazing fire. He wears a golden crown. Beside him is a shield bearing the sign of an eagle. He holds a scepter, the symbol of his great power.

The Emperor says to you, "I am the great principles; I am action, I am completion, and I am result; I am the great law."

The Emperor says to you:

I am your _____

I will give you _____

Your password is _____

With this password you can _____

My message for you is _____

The Emperor is the king, the father figure who rules as a powerful but benevolent dictator. He represents confidence, assertion, authority, and achievement. The message and password are your own manifestations of confidence, authority, and achievement.

Say to yourself:
I have will and power, discipline and ambition to meet all of my highest goals.

Looking at . . .

The Sword

magine you see a sword on the road in front of you.

What does the sword look like? _____

How do you feel about it? _____

What will you do with it? _____

Where did it come from? _____

To whom does it belong? _____

What color is it? _____

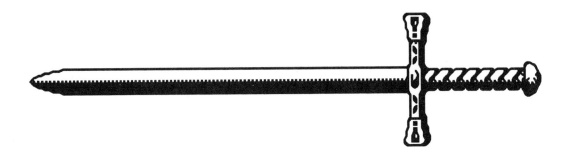

The sword is a symbol of power, strength, courage, authority, and leadership. Your answers to the exercise of the sword indicate your feelings about these attributes. Are you comfortable with the sword? Does it belong to you? If not, close your eyes and imagine the sword with your name engraved on the hilt; it is your own symbol of power and strength, and you are armed with it as you travel the mysterious roads ahead.

Looking at . . .

The Crown

You have come across a crown along the path.

What does it look like? _____

What is it made of? _____

How do you feel about it? _____

What will you do with it? _____

To whom does it belong? _____

The crown represents victory, dignity, sovereignty, and reward, the highest attainment. Did you put it on? If not, what have you learned about your feelings about success? Close your eyes and imagine you are wearing the crown . . . feel your power.

Looking at . . .

The Throne

You have come to a great throne. You climb up to it and sit down on it.

How do you feel? _____

What do you do? _____

_____

The throne is the seat of authority, knowledge, and rule. Are you comfortable sitting there? If not, spend a few minutes imagining yourself sitting on a throne that was made especially for you, with your initials inscribed on it. As you sit on it you have a sense of great strength; you are able to tap your unlimited power.

Order and Reason

he great Greek god Zeus was the protector, the ruler, and the representative of the Olympic order. His rule was absolute over gods and men.

Like Zeus, the Emperor represents law and order, authority, and paternity over the material world. He is still very much with us and his rule affects our society even today. We are all familiar with the authoritative rule of the system, which, in its excess, is suspicious of independent, creative innovation and favors conformity to the prevailing order.

What can we learn from the Emperor? We know his powers and we also see his excesses; in fact, they may be our own. We all subject ourselves to rules, schedules, and calendars, sometimes at the expense of our spontaneity and creativity, sometimes even our humanity. The Emperor represents personal power, but he also stands as a warning against creating a world in which all reality is regulated and all truth is measurable, tangible, and quantitative.

An understanding of the necessity for limiting the powers of the Emperor can be seen in the following quote from the Chinese philosopher Lao-tzu regarding the Tao and Wu Wei (conformity to the Tao). The ruler is cautioned to avoid arrogance as well as violence and to be flexible.

When a magistrate follows the Tao he has no need to resort to force of arms to strengthen the Empire, because his business methods alone will show good returns. Briars and thorns grow rank where an army camps. But harvests are the sequence of a great war. The good ruler will be resolute, and then stop, he dare not take by force. One should be resolute, but not boastful; resolute but not arrogant; resolute but yielding when it cannot be avoided; resolute but he must not resort to violence. With a resort to force, things flourish for a time, but then decay.

The Emperor and the Ego

ur personal interpretations of our experiences constitute authoritative messages that are accepted without reservation by the passive subconscious mind. Thus, in a sense each of us is the Emperor. We make our own laws, define our own realities, and then find ourselves acting within the constraints of our interpretations of reality.

The authoritative aspect of the ego can be seen in the mythologic figure of Zeus, who may be in danger of becoming overwhelmed by his ego as he attempts to force his will on every aspect of the environment. If we can shift our attention away from the ego, away from the confines of our absorption with the self, which is our usual preoccupation when we are thinking of the literal mode ("How do I look? Do they like me? Am I more successful than he is?"), we suddenly open ourselves to a whole new world of meaning.

We are all searching for a sense of meaningfulness in our lives. Albert Einstein once said, "What is the meaning of life? To find a satisfactory answer to that question is to become religious." The realm in which we will find answers in our search for meaningfulness must go beyond the literal and beyond the self, and beyond the realms of the Emperor.

The Emperor rules our world with authority and wisdom. He represents the powers of our culture in its scientific and technical splendor. But we can find our own truth only when we look inside.

The Soul Lost in the Age of Technology

f we were to think of ourselves as nothing more than complicated supercomputers, we would ignore our inner lives, our meanings, and our souls. When we assume that reality is what advertisers say it is in commercials and glossy ads, our framework of belief becomes focused on externals. There is less inside as we focus more energy on what goes on outside. Finally, we end up with no coherent overall sense of meaning or purpose in life, living in a vacuum in which everything is OK until the machines are turned off. Then, late at night when we are all alone, we find ourselves face-to-face with the terrifying void. With no inner significance we are doomed to constantly grasp for external answers, which turn out to be merely illusions.

Inside us is a realm that haunts our dreams and controls our lives in subtle ways, but we have left it unexplored. Maybe we are experts at the jobs we do during the day, but the hidden half of our minds, the inner workings, remain more mysterious than ever.

Among primitive tribes, people pray to a god of the lake or a god of fertility, and they find meaning all around them. But if our only god is the coin of the realm, we will constantly feel disappointed and let down. The literal world has imprisoned our ability to dream, and life feels empty. Some anthropologists tell us that without a fundamental sense of meaning, the human organism often does not fulfill its essential biological functions.

If we invest all our hopes and dreams in another person, a place, or a thing, we are invariably disappointed and disillusioned. Our personal salvation cannot come from outside ourselves. Rather, a sense of salvation comes from our relationship with our inner self, and it belongs to the world of the soul.

Chapter 6
The Hierophant

he Hierophant represents the saintly, religious aspect of the psyche. He is the high priest, the rabbi, or the pope. He sits between two columns holding a cross in his left hand. Two keys lie at his feet.

Looking at . . .

The Hierophant

 he great master is sitting in the temple. He wears the robes of a spiritual leader. His face is serene and his eyes are penetrating as he looks at you. You feel the magnitude of his presence; you know this is truly a saintly man.

The holy man says to you, "Look for the path that leads inward; follow the truth and find the treasures from within."

The Hierophant says to you:

The first truth is _____

_____

The miracle is _____

_____

Your pathway leads to _____

_____

The keys at the Hierophant's feet are from the sun and the moon. They can unlock

_____

which is kept _____

_____

The Hierophant represents the blessings of intuitive guidance. The path is your way to self-fulfillment. The words of the Hierophant are messages to you from your own intuition.

Say to yourself:
I am guided and directed by my highest wisdom for
the greatest good, in myself and in the world.

Looking at . . .

The Key

 magine you have found an old key by the side of the road.

What does it look like? _____

How do you feel about it? _____

Where did it come from? _____

To whom does it belong? _____

What will it unlock? _____

What will you do with it? _____

The key symbolizes knowledge. Your response to the questions about the key will give you some understanding of the role of wisdom in your life.

The Story of John-Baptist Vianney

ohn Vianney was the son of a French peasant farmer. His studies for the priesthood were slow and unpromising, but eventually he was ordained, more because of his devoutness and goodwill than for any other qualifications.

The newly ordained father was sent to a lonely and neglected village as the parish priest. There he devoted his heart and soul to his parishioners. Soon Father Vianney came to be known as a gifted preacher and confessor. Villagers from miles around began to talk about the country priest's gifts and powers.

Soon the isolated village became a place of pilgrimage for tens of thousands of people who came from all over France and beyond. Year after year, Father Vianney spent up to eighteen hours a day in the confessional. He had extraordinary powers of insight and understanding. It was even said that he was able to tell about distant and future events.

Some of the other clergy complained to the bishop about Father Vianney's work, calling him a madman and a charlatan. Finally, the bishop said to them, "I wish, gentlemen, that all my clergy had a touch of the same madness."[6]

Father Vianney had extraordinary powers of insight and understanding.

The Story of the Priest at St. Sophia

 popular early Christian tradition relates that at the moment an invading Turkish army entered the great Byzantine church of St. Sophia, a liturgy was being celebrated. The priest who held the holy sacrament saw the Muslim army rush into the church. Miraculously, the altar wall opened in front of him. He entered and disappeared within.

The tradition says that when Constantinople (modern-day Istanbul) is once again in the hands of the Christians, the priest will come out from the altar wall and continue the liturgy.[7]

The priest, or Hierophant, represents the link between God and man through the ritual creed and ceremony of formalized religion. The priest is a guide in our striving for transcendent meaning; he is a symbol of our search for a connection with God and an aid for making this connection.

I have just recovered the key of the lost staircase . . . The staircase in the wall . . . winds from the subterranean depths of the Ego to the high terraces crowned by the stars.

Romain Rolland

Looking at . . .

The Opening in the Floor

Imagine there is an opening in the center of the floor in your room.

How deep is the hole? _____

How far down can you see? _____

Imagine you climb down through the hole. What do you see? _____

_____

When you reach the bottom, what do you find? _____

Finish these sentences:

I feel _____

I wish _____

I will _____

I need _____

I fear _____

I secretly _____

Imagine there is a hole in the floor . . .

Looking at . . .

The Opening in the Sky

magine you look up and see an opening in the sky.

What do you see? _____

How do you feel about it? _____

How big is the hole? _____

You can see up through the opening. What lies beyond? _____

Now picture yourself going up through the opening. How do you feel? _____

What do you see? _____

When you have ascended, finish these sentences:

I feel _____

I am _____

I must _____

I have _____

I believe _____

Imagine you look up and see an opening in the sky . . .

The opening in the floor represents the descent into the unconscious. The way you feel about it will affect your willingness to explore your inner regions; the sentences you finished show your innermost feelings about your descent.

If you are uncomfortable or afraid of going down into the hole in the floor, imagine you go down again, this time knowing that great gifts and guidance await you and that you are safe and welcome.

The opening in the sky represents your spiritual vision, your ascent into the realms of God. The way you feel about this ascent reflects your sense of spirituality. It shows how you feel about God and spiritual transcendence.

If you are afraid of going up through this opening, imagine your angel is with you to guide you and show you the things that are in heaven.

The Vision

n the story about the priest at St. Sophia, the priest could not be overcome or destroyed. When external forms of the faith are invaded, the priest, who represents our own striving for a connectedness with God, withdraws inward into the altar or into a sacred place within the self. There it will remain, listening to the sounds of the inner voice, until it is safe and free once again to act out the rituals and symbols of its faith.

The inner voice provides the vision that can give us answers and solutions to make sense of our lives. The vision, which is the source of our inner quest, comes from intuition and from our imagination, not from literal outward manifestations. It is, rather, that dynamic image which we can accept and believe in wholeheartedly that can change even our most hopeless situations into important opportunities for growth and advancement. Finding this vision and learning to follow it is the significance of the symbol of the Hierophant.

*A vision that we believe in completely can change any
situation into an opportunity for growth.*

Carl Jung said that when we feel weak, the inner center will supply us with images that are right at any moment to give us a sense of order and meaning.

The search for a sense of direction and purpose will lead us to the world of the psyche, which goes beyond words.

Going Beyond Words

he world that exists past our words is where images and symbols express the ineffable. By understanding these images and interacting with them through techniques that use visualization and imagery, we can begin to identify and participate in all aspects of our lives in new, rich ways.

An experience that seems pointless when participated in on a literal level can become alive and important when we participate in it fully, when we look for its spiritual significance.

When we visualize an image rather than just looking at the object itself or at a picture, all of the symbolic content of that image becomes personal and at the same time universal. It comes to represent something about our own experience; it becomes a metaphor for some aspect of our lives.

When we view them literally, we may note certain interesting recurring themes in fairy tales and myths. But when we are able to recognize these themes as metaphors for the life experiences we all share, they suddenly possess a personal and compelling significance. These are the stories of our dreams. By understanding them, we can begin to understand the inner complexities that determine who we are and how we will live.

This, too, is the power an image takes when it is internalized, which is what happens when we use our imagination to inwardly visualize a picture. The picture we imagine becomes a part of ourselves and part of our experience.

The techniques of visualization can be used effectively for making significant improvements in our lives. Visualization may be used, among other things, to:

- Enrich our personal understanding of ourselves and our needs

- Expand our limitations and boundaries

- Review and learn from past events

- Develop new strengths and abilities

- Enhance our creative and intuitive processes

- Create a sense of confidence and of being centered

The Ceremony of Initiation

his is the point at which you must confront the issues you have with regard to your mother and father. The four sages—the High Priestess, the Empress, the Emperor, and the Hierophant—are the symbolic figures who will provide you with an understanding of your parents.

Which of these figures best represents your mother? _____

Why? _____

Your mother has this message for you:

Her regret is _____

Her gift to you is _____

Which of these figures best represents your father? _____

Why? _____

Your father has this message for you: _____

His regret is _____

His gift to you is _____

The blessing from your parents is _____

In order for you to become initiated as the hero you must _____

_____

Step II in Review

During Step II of your travels you met with four sages, who represent four different aspects of your own psyche, two feminine and two masculine. They have provided you with the information and insights of your initiation into the role of the hero of the quest. Write a short summary of the most important aspects of your experience so far.

Write down the most important feeling and insights you have gained from your travels through this second stage, your initiation.

Step III
Withdrawal

You have been initiated. You have met with the sages and you have learned from them.
Now you must withdraw within yourself, to find your center and your balance. The next
four chapters will lead you through the withdrawal portion of your pilgrimage.

Chapter 7
The Lovers

he symbol of the Lovers represents the harmony of the two sides, the right and left, the male and female, the yin and yang. This image represents unity and the synthesis of opposites in compassionate, loving intimacy.

Looking at . . .

The Lovers

he Lovers stand on a green hillside before a tall mountain. Their love is both a sacrifice and a prayer through which the magic of existence is opened. They represent the unification and integration of opposites into the whole each lacks separately.

The woman gazes upward, where she gains inspiration. She says:

I am_____

I can _____

I have _____

I will _____

The man gazes at the woman. He says:

The dark cloud between us represents_____

I will _____

The message from the Angel of the Air is

_____

_____

The Lovers represent the coming together of opposites. This can only happen when there is a recognition and a respect for duality, and a mutual cooperation. This is the agreement of the conscious and the subconscious minds.

The dark cloud represents the basis of difficulty in your own personal process of growth and synthesis. The Angel of the Air represents a divine messenger; what did you learn from her?

The male/female androgyne is a symbol of perfection and wholeness in the union of the male and female forces in which the opposites—heaven and earth, night and day, mother and father—are united.

Say to yourself:
I am in harmony and a state of balance with both the feminine and the masculine parts of myself, and with my consciousness and my unconscious. Therefore I am in harmonious balance within myself and with others.

Looking at . . .

The Circle and the Square

What symbol or picture would represent a sense of the material world for you? Write it in the box.

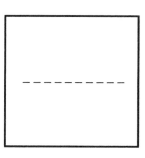 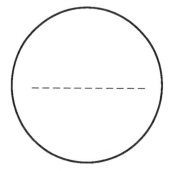

What would represent the spirit for you? Write it in the circle.

In your mind, imagine the merging of these two symbols. Try to hold the image.

What does this new, combined image say to you? _____

_____

This exercise will help you find a mental balance between the material and the spiritual realms. Use the message of the new, combined image when you feel the need to refocus.

Balancing the material and the spiritual realms is the pathway to inner harmony.

Looking at . . .

The Mirror

Imagine you are looking into a magical mirror. What do you see? _____

_____

How do you feel about the image in the mirror? _____

Imagine that the mirror image finishes these sentences:

I am _____

I can _____

I will _____

I must _____

I secretly _____

In the Greek myth, the Gorgon Medusa could only be looked at through a mirror; looking at her directly would turn men to stone. Most mere mortals cannot look at the gods, or at truth, directly.

Often what we see in life or in other people is actually a reflection of ourselves, our fears and inadequacies. We can see past these illusions when we free ourselves from the confines of the ego and remove ourselves from the world of appearances. Then we can be free to explore the full dimensions of our real selves, instead of just the limitations of our reflections.

Think about your reflection in the mirror and what it means to you.

Looking at . . .

The Mountaintop

Imagine you have been climbing a tall mountain.

What is the best way for you to reach the top? _____

When you finally reach the top of the mountain, what do you see? _____

_____

How do you feel? _____

What do you do? _____

What do you find? _____

What can you see as you look over to the other side of the mountain? _____

_____

*The figure on top of the mountain has achieved
fulfillment with the help of the angel.*

Ascent to the mountaintop represents the attainment of the whole and
unlimited from the partial, limited, and unfulfilled. It is success and fulfillment. The other side of the mountain is the future.

The Myth of Eros and Psyche

The Greek myth of the lovers Eros (love) and Psyche (the soul) is a metaphorical variation on the beauty-and-the-beast theme.

Psyche was the beautiful daughter of a king. She was far more beautiful than her two sisters. However, her sisters soon found husbands, while Psyche remained in her father's house, without suitors. The king, despairing of ever finding a husband for her, consulted an oracle. The oracle told him to abandon psyche on the top of a mountain where she would be taken off by a monster. The king and queen were in anguish, but they had to obey this decree because they were told it was the will of the gods, whom they feared to disobey.

Aphrodite, the goddess of love, was jealous of Psyche. For revenge she ordered

The wind carried Psyche to a beautiful castle

her son, Eros, to make Psyche fall in love with a poor, ugly monster. But when Eros saw Psyche, he fell in love with her himself.

Psyche was led to the mountaintop to be abandoned, but instead of being taken away by a monster, the wind Zephyrus lifted Psyche gently off to a beautiful castle where she was attended by invisible servants. Lovely voices waited on her, fed her, and amused her by day. At night, in the darkness, the husband the oracle had told of joined her. He did not seem to be a monster, but Psyche could not see him.

Every morning her husband would fly away, to join her again the next night. Psyche was happy but lonely, so she persuaded her husband to allow her sisters to visit her. He warned her of the danger of her nostalgia, but she begged and he finally agreed.

The wind Zephyrus brought Psyche's sisters to the palace. They were bitterly jealous to see the splendor of the castle where their sister lived, and they convinced her to find out what her husband looked like.

Unable to overcome her own curiosity, and at the insistence of her sisters, Psyche hid a knife and a lamp in her room so that she could see and kill her monster husband. But when Psyche saw her beautiful husband, she realized he was the god Eros. In her amazement and fright, she spilled a drop of boiling oil from her lamp on him. When he awoke and saw what she had done, he flew off at once, never to return.

Months passed. Brokenhearted, Psyche decided to find her husband. First she punished her sisters by telling them that Eros asked to see them. Delighted, they jumped off a cliff, thinking that Zephyrus the wind waited to carry them off. Instead they fell to the ravine below.

Psyche traveled throughout the world searching for Eros, but her efforts were in vain. Finally she went to Aphrodite, who tortured her and then sent her off to the underworld to bring back a box of beauty ointment. Psyche was told not to open the box, but she could not resist. When she opened it a sleep vapor escaped and she fell unconscious.

However, Eros was desperately in love with Psyche. When he saw her in the magic sleep, he wakened her and went to Zeus to ask for permission to marry a mortal. Zeus gave his consent and finally Aphrodite and Psyche were reconciled. Later, Eros and Psyche had a beautiful child, whom they named Pleasure.

This story can be seen as a description of the soul, or Psyche, which is beautiful but corruptible until it has undergone the tests that will make it worthy, aided by the power of love, or Eros. The two lovers can be seen as the two different aspects of the self, the soul and the worldly outer person, which can be united as lovers after corruptions, pettinesses, and vanities are overcome.

This philosophical egg represents the union of the opposites, which triumphs over chaos and the dragon. The seven planets represent seven stages of transformation and seven aspects of the personality.

Dreams and Images

n dreams the psyche is fragmented into many parts. These various parts are connected by scenes and stories. We learn from dreams about the true nature of the psyche and the nature of psychic reality, which deals not in terms of *I* but of *we*, not of one but of many.

Dreams free us from our identity with the ego of the waking state, which is represented in the myth by Psyche's sisters. This freedom allows us to experience a greater truth than we are ever able to know when we are thinking rationally and literally. But our dreams are largely inaccessible. We often forget them or we are unable to understand them.

Any type of visual imagery has the same attendant sensations and effects as the actual situation, whether it is a dream or a waking visualization. Because our dreams are often difficult to remember and to understand, we can learn to use other kinds of images to uncover the hidden facets of the self.

Certain images and symbols have a great deal of meaning to our unconscious minds. They constitute the inner, primary language that exists before feelings are translated into words. By learning this language of symbols and images, we can establish a dialogue with the hidden part of ourselves we often ignore or misunderstand. Communicating with our unconscious minds can provide a powerful resource for defining and reaching our goals.

Visual imagery, imagining something and seeing it in the mind, can be a wonderful tool for controlling our moods and even our health. If we visualize something negative in our minds, the resulting mood and feelings will be negative. If, on the other hand, we visualize something positive, our disposition will be positive. By learning the techniques of visualization we can discover a great source of inner power and a medium as rich as our dreams for self-understanding.

Obviously if one part of ourselves is aiming in one direction and the other, the hidden part, for reasons as inscrutable as our dreams, is heading off in the opposite direction, we will exist in a perpetual state of inner conflict.

If, however, our outer, rational functions and our inner, intuitive impulses are in agreement about their mutual goals and objectives, we will have dramatically increased our prospects for success, happiness, and health.

With the whole system in agreement and striving for common objectives, a new strength and power will suddenly become available to us. Considering that there are billions of brain cells that are never used in the lifetime of even the most brilliant and accomplished human being, it is not at all unreasonable for us to expect that we can become capable of undreamed-of accomplishments when we learn to communicate with our inner minds.

The king and queen are in harmony. The eagle represents spiritual inspiration. The lions are the soul and the spirit.

The alchemical picture above portrays the Lovers, or the union of opposites, with two lions that symbolize the soul and the spirit. They must be united in their body; the soul and spirit must become one in the heart.

The hermaphrodite, or androgyne, also represents this conjunction, this bringing together of opposites. The sun is male and the moon female. Together they form a figure of perfection in whom the soul and spirit are merged into one. When these opposites are brought together, the body (or material world) becomes spiritualized, and the spirit becomes expressed in practical terms, like morality and goodness.

Chapter 8
The Chariot

he Chariot represents that part of the self whose power lies in self-control and self-discipline. It stands for victory over the instincts, and self-mastery, which leads to conquest and triumph.

Looking at . . .

The Charioteer

 he Charioteer stands ready; he is in control of himself and his life. He drives a team of two creatures. Imagine yourself as the Charioteer.

What are the creatures that pull your chariot? _____

What is the direction of your efforts? _____

The Charioteer says:

My strength is _____

I am _____

I can _____

I have _____

My weakness is _____

I am hiding the _____

The direction I will take is _____

Plato described the soul as a winged chariot drawn by two horses representing contrary aspects of human nature, the one striving upward, the other pulling downward.

The qualities of the chariot driver are symbolized by the type of team driven. In Norse mythology, Freyja drives a chariot drawn by cats to represent a lunar and magical journey. White horses can represent spirituality and purity. The human-headed sphinx suggests the human spirit overcoming animal instincts, or the union of intellectual and physical powers.

Say to yourself:
By harnessing all my efforts
toward my goal, I will be victorious.

Looking at . . . *The Mask*

magine yourself wearing a mask.

What does the mask look like? _____

How do you feel about the mask? _____

Do you want to take it off? _____ Why? _____

The mask says:

I am _____

I can _____

I will _____

I feel _____

I must _____

I have _____

The mask represents protection and concealment. Wearing the mask of a specific character can represent an identification with it, or a concealment of yourself behind it. Animal or bird masks represent communion with nature and instinctual wisdom.

The mask you wear may be an indication of your way of hiding from your problems, from yourself, or from the world. The message of the Charioteer is that you dont need to hide; you can triumph over adversity through self-control and self-discipline.

Looking at . . .

The Three Boxes

This visualization exercise uses the geometric symbol from Pythagoras' proof that the area of a square is equal to the area of two smaller squares built upon a right triangle, and vice versa. Symbolically this shows that the triangle is a perfect figure, because it contains and will support all that is built upon it.

Visualize three boxes, a small one, a medium-sized one, and a large one.

What color is the small box? _____

What color is the medium-sized box? _____

What color is the large box?_____

Look in the small box. What do you find? _____

Imagine that the contents of the small box completes the following sentences:

I am _____

I wish _____

I must _____

I need _____

I feel _____

I secretly _____

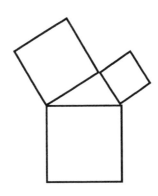

Look in the medium-sized box.

What is inside? _____

Imagine that the contents of the medium-sized box completes the following sentences:

I am _____

I wish _____

I feel _____

I secretly _____

What is inside the large box? Imagine that the contents of the large box completes the following sentences:

I am _____

I wish _____

I feel _____

I secretly _____

Now imagine that the contents of all three boxes meet.

What happens? _____

The small box represents the inner you. The middle box is your personality, the conscious you. The large box represents your outer self, the public you. The relationship among these three images reflects the way these three parts of yourself interact.

If you visualized conflict among the contents of the three boxes, close your eyes and imagine all the contents of the boxes together in a harmonious relationship.

The Myth of Theseus

T he ancient Greek hero Theseus, who was the son of a queen and two fathers, a king and the god Poseidon, can be said to represent the Charioteer. On one of his heroic exploits Theseus slew the monster Minotaur.

On the island of Crete, seven young boys and seven virgin girls were to be sacrificed as food for the Minotaur. Theseus set out to destroy the monster. When he arrived at Crete, Princess Ariadne, the daughter of King Minos the ruler of the island, fell in love with him. Ariadne gave Theseus a ball of string so he could find his way back out of the labyrinth in which the Minotaur was kept. Theseus slew the beast and escaped the labyrinth. Then he left Crete, taking Princess Ariadne with him, as well as her sister Phaedra. But on the way home, Theseus abandoned Ariadne on the island of Naxos.

Before he had sailed for Crete, Theseus had promised his father that he would put up a white flag if he had been successful in killing the Minotaur. If he failed, his ship would fly a black flag. Theseus forgot his promise to change the flag on the way home. Seeing the black flag, his father believed his son was dead. In his despair, he threw himself into the sea.

Theseus, like the Charioteer, was heroic in facing his task through his strength and courage. However, he abandoned Ariadne, and later, because of Theseus' thoughtlessness, his father killed himself.

This myth and the symbol of the Charioteer both seem to show us that strength and power are virtues that serve us in meeting the trials and adversities of life. But alone these virtues are not sufficient to ensure a fully victorious outcome. They must be tempered with other attributes, such as a respect for the feelings and needs of others and a sense of integrity in personal relationships.

Freyja drives a chariot drawn by cats, which represent her inner powers.

Reflections . . .

Through the Labyrinth

nner virtues and values that can guide the Charioteer come from listening to the wisdom from within.

Theseus' guide out of the labyrinth was a simple ball of string. No type of weapon could have served him. The string represents our instincts and intuition. The labyrinth is our own inner self, and the Minotaur is all our negative thoughts and fears. We, like the hero, can slay our monsters, but only with the help of our inner, intuitive faculties. When we return from the labyrinth, we will discover that we have glimpsed some unknown component that makes meaning possible, that turns empty events into important experiences and gives our lives a new significance.

Unfortunately, however, once we are safely back from the labyrinth, we are often tempted to abandon those very processes that led us safely through, just as Theseus abandoned Ariadne. The resources that guide us through the maze are the images, fantasies, and symbols from the unconscious. Our conscious mind may try to define what we experience inside the labyrinth, but words are a dim reflection of the actual experience. A whole nonverbal language exists in the unconscious. It is a visual language of form and symbol that uses shapes, colors, and pictures instead of words.

Think about the nature of your own labyrinth and the monster that lurks within. Imagine a symbol that represents your liberation from the maze.

Universal Symbols

S ymbols are the nonverbal language of the unconscious mind. Some symbols are cultural, such as a flag or a monument. Some are religious, such as the cross and the Star of David.

There are also what Carl Jung called universal symbols. These symbols will elicit the same response from any person no matter what culture he or she comes from. For instance, a dark cloud is a natural symbol suggesting all that we associate with a storm.

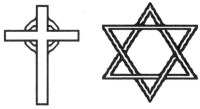

According to Jung, symbols are the basic universal language inherent in the structure of the human brain. Symbols are a part of our primal experience. Of course, the effect a symbol will have on someone will vary from person to person. It will also vary from one time to another, depending upon how the person is feeling. But certain generalizations prevail that are consistent for anyone who views a universal symbol.

Color is one important form of symbolism. Each color represents certain attitudes and feelings and will elicit particular responses. In fact, color has been observed to cause actual physiological changes in people. When one is exposed to the color red, for instance, the blood pressure, electrical conductance of the skin, respiration rate, eye blinks, and brain-wave patterns increase. On the other hand, when one is exposed to the color blue, the body becomes relaxed and tranquil.

Symbols and images are our only meaningful means of expression for inner experiences. We can attempt to translate them into words, but in order to completely recall and understand our feelings we must be able to retain a memory of them through images. This is the reason that poetry and mythology, which utilize metaphors, symbolism, and imagery, can be so moving for us. If we tried to interpret them as fact, whether historical, biographical, or literal, their meaning would be diluted. The only way to understand images is by seeking their meaning intuitively.

We use symbols for many things that go beyond the range of human understanding. They represent concepts we cannot quite define or fully comprehend. The symbol is a picture that bridges the outer world and the inner. In the world of symbols, the specific represents the universal. Things like a feeling of rebirth, or the idea of the meaning of life, or fate, are concepts we all understand and share, but they do not fit into any rational system. They cannot be pinned down. They can only be understood symbolically. Symbols serve to unify fragmented ideas and feelings, and they allow us to glimpse things we could never understand otherwise.

In many ancient cultures the people saw spirit gods in rivers and trees. They prayed to the spirits, and they depicted their visions of the gods in drawings and sculptures. They were close to nature and to creative expression, and they were accustomed to acting out their symbolic realities. Theirs was a world in which the powers of nature and the powers of prayer were vital parts of everyday life. The seasons and the rituals connected with them gave the people a sense of their place in the scheme of things; they experienced a harmony between the inner and outer worlds. This is the balance we are missing. We have learned to manipulate the outer world, but we have abandoned the inner world in the process.

The subconscious mind, which exists below the level of conscious thought, is passive but powerful. It can make us sick or cure us. It can make us rich or destroy us. We are angels or devils depending on the state of our unconscious mind, where the thoughts we repress and the feelings we are not aware of are hidden. This is why it is so important that we learn its language. In order for it to work on our behalf, we must communicate our wishes to the unconscious, which will then give us control of ourselves and thus of our lives. Once in control, we can take charge of the vehicle of our being to guide ourselves through the experiences of existence.

The driver of the chariot represents the mind or spirit directing the body through life. Its message is that instead of being tossed about by life, we can learn to master it.

Chapter 9
Strength

he symbol of Strength represents the vital energy of the higher self. This strength comes from using the positive energy of the spirit, which has the power to overcome our lower impulses.

Looking at . . .

Strength

The lion is subdued by the woman. She has the strength to endure despite all obstacles; she has the determination, the stamina, the courage, and the energy to succeed. She represents freedom from repression through perseverance and vitality. She has a passionate enthusiasm for life.

The woman who subdues the lion looks at you. You are infused with a vigorous sense of your own power and strength. She asks you to write down a difficulty or

a problem that has been of concern to you: _____

_____

You can control the lion by _____

The lion represents your _____

You must _____

You can _____

What will you gain by harnessing the lion? _____

The woman tells you to remember _____

Her warning is that _____

> The woman uses her love of life as her source of strength, as she harnesses the energy of the beast. She has learned to assimilate its power and use it as her own. This gives her the will to succeed. She represents your ability to control the beast so that it is no longer a threat to you.

The lion represents the drive for power, which we can learn to convert into spiritual energy.

Say to yourself:
I release the energy from my greatest fears, weaknesses, and repressions,
and utilize it as a source of vitality and power, which enables me
to reach my highest dreams.

Looking at . . .

The Lion

Imagine that a lion stands before you.

It says _____

Then it tells you that _____

The lion says:

I am _____

I will _____

I can give you _____

I always _____

How do you feel about the lion? _____

The lion represents strength and power, which you can utilize for personal growth.

Looking at . . .

Ways of Looking

Look outside and find a tree. Look at the tree as a botanical specimen. Think of it in terms of its categories; is it evergreen or deciduous, young or old, strong or weak? Is it larger or smaller than others you have seen of its kind? How does it compare with the other trees around it?

Describe the tree: _____

_____

Close your eyes. Then look at the tree again, but this time look at it as though you had never seen a tree before. Notice the way the light shines on its leaves, and how the leaves move in the wind. See the colors and shapes of the tree. Try to perceive it directly, emotionally, allowing yourself to experience your feelings about the tree. Pretend for a moment that you are the tree; feel a tree-knowingness throughout your mind and body.

Describe the tree the way it looks to you now: _____

_____

_____

Looking at . . .

Two Ways of Seeing

The next time you are in a grocery store, think about your shopping list and concentrate on the items you have come to buy. Examine the objects you need, comparing ingredients and quantities listed on the labels. Think about the packaging—does it effectively represent the product? Think about the relative prices and which product is the best value.

Close your eyes and pause for a moment. Now try to imagine the store as a whole. Open your eyes and look at the light as it penetrates the aisles. Notice the temperature of the room. Become aware of the smells around you. Look at the colors and textures of the boxes, packages, and produce. Listen to the sounds—the people, the background music, the machinery, the intercom system. Feel the environment, become a part of it.

Now separate yourself from the surroundings.

Compare the two experiences. (You might want to write down your insights in your journal.)

Anything you do in life can be goal-oriented and fact-centered, or it can be a sensory stimulation. Try the two modes of perception the next time you are in a crowd of people, or at the zoo, or out in nature. With practice you can learn to decide at will which mode to use and select the one best suited to the moment, instead of being trapped into a half-awareness using only one part of your faculties.

Look for the beauty all around you and the beauty will become a part of you.

Looking at . . .

The Eye

Sit in a relaxed position, breathing evenly. Close your eyes and imagine there is an eye in the middle of your forehead. Picture the eye clearly.

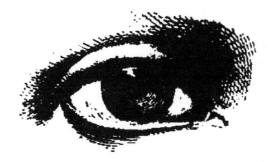

The eye says to you:

I am your _____

I can _____

I will _____

I see _____

I remember _____

I secretly _____

I know that _____

> The eye represents the faculty of intuitive vision, enlightenment, and omni-science.

The Story of Molly Whuppie

nce there was a man and wife who had so many children they could not feed them all. So the man took his three youngest daughters into the deep forest and left them there.

The girls wandered through the woods all night until they saw the lights of a house ahead. They went to the house and asked if they could stay the night.

The woman of the house told the children she could not let them stay because her husband was a giant, and he would kill them if he found them. But the girls were so tired they begged her, "Please let us stay and rest. We can leave before the giant gets home."

So the woman let them in and sat them down before the great fire with some bread and milk. Just as they sat down, the giant arrived at the door. "Fee fie fo fum, I smell the blood of an earthly one," the giant bellowed.

"It is just three homeless girls, let them stay the night," the wife pleaded. Finally the giant agreed.

The giant had his supper and then he told the three girls they were to share a bed with his own three daughters. Before bed, he tied a straw rope around the neck of each of the three homeless children and he put a gold chain around the neck of each of his own daughters.

The youngest child, who was called Molly Whuppie, felt uneasy about the rope around her neck and the necks of her sisters, so she stayed awake when the rest fell asleep. When all the house was quiet, she took off the straw ropes and put them around the necks of the giant's daughters. She put the gold chains on herself and her sisters. Then she lay down again.

Late in the night, the giant rose and took the girls with the ropes around their necks and beat them to death. Molly woke her sisters, and they ran back into the woods as fast as they could. Soon they came to a large castle, where they asked permission to stay.

Molly told the king about her adventure with the giant. The king said, "Molly, you are a clever girl. If you go back and bring me the giant's magic sword, your eldest sister shall wed my eldest son."

"I will try," Molly said. So she went back to the giant's house and silently stole his sword. But the giant awoke and chased her through the forest. Molly ran until she reached the Bridge of One Hair. She ran over it, but the giant was too big and could not follow.

When Molly took the giant's sword to the king, her oldest sister was married to the king's eldest son.

Then the king said, "Molly, you are a clever girl. If you go back to the giant's house and bring me his purse of gold, your middle sister will marry my middle son."

"I will try," said Molly. She returned to the giant's house, and while he was sound asleep she stole his purse of gold. But before she could escape, he awoke and chased her through the forest until she reached the Bridge of One Hair. Again Molly crossed, but the giant was too big and could not follow.

When she gave the king the giant's purse of gold, he said, "Molly, you are a clever girl. If you can get the giant's ring from his finger, you will wed my youngest son."

"I will try," said Molly. She returned once again to the giant's house, and when he was sound asleep she pulled his ring from his finger. But the giant awoke and caught her.

The lion represents the passionate, devouring drive for power.
When this drive is material instead of spiritual, it becomes destructive.

"What would you do if you caught a thief stealing your ring?" the giant asked Molly. Clever Molly answered, "I would put him in a sack with the cat and dog and hang him on a hook while I went to the woods to find a club. Then I would beat him with it."

"And that is just what I will do with you!" he exclaimed. He put Molly in a sack with the cat and dog and he hung her on a hook and left to find a club.

While he was gone, Molly sang out, "Oh, this is so pretty!"

The giant's wife begged Molly to show her what was so pretty. Molly told her to cut a hole in the sack and climb in. As the wife climbed in, Molly climbed out. Then she sewed up the hole in the sack and hid behind the door.

Soon the giant returned with a huge club and struck the sack. His wife yelled out, "Stop it! It's me in here!" But the cat and dog made so much noise the giant could not hear her.

Then Molly, who did not want the giant to seriously hurt the woman, stepped out from behind the door. The giant chased her to the Bridge of One Hair. Molly crossed, but the giant was too big and could not follow.

When she returned to the castle, Molly and the youngest prince were married. Molly never saw the giant again.

In this story, Molly's strength and courage enable her to overcome the giant, or the primitive animal nature in herself (or in humankind). She takes the giant's sword, his coins, and his ring—the magical sources of his power, which she will transform into positive energy for her own use. The girl is not destroyed by the giant; instead she finds methods for utilizing his resources in new, positive ways for her own life.

The symbol of Strength represents the sacrifices of the ego and self-awareness—which becomes lust, greed, and other primitive drives—for spiritual inner forces that can be liberating and powerful. The capacities of the spirit will help us tame the lower animal instincts that rule us.

The demons in this illustration represent the lower animal instincts, or the seven deadly sins (anger, avarice, envy, gluttony, pride, lust, and sloth).

In the picture below, the lion is devouring the sun. This symbolizes the violent passions that can overwhelm the consciousness. When the drive for power (the lion) focuses on a materialistic level, its force is corrupted. It becomes a vice and therefore destructive. But when the passion is spiritual, this symbol represents personal transformation and resurrection. This is the chapter of Strength, in which the devouring energy of the lion is overcome and used as a vital positive energy for life.

The lion devouring the sun represents the consciousness of the self, which can overwhelm violent desires.

Reflections . . .

Using Words to Distance Ourselves from the World

 n the picture of Strength at the beginning of this chapter, the woman uses her spiritual, inner resources to come to terms with her own lower impulses. She does not seek to destroy these impulses; rather she will subdue them and learn to convert their power in order to use it for higher purposes of her own. She can do this through the powers of her spiritual nature, by feeling and experiencing life directly, without attempting to analyze or manipulate it.

This is the process that belongs to the world of creativity and inspiration, where the viewer and the object somehow blend. This is the experience we have when we imagine or visualize something, and the thing we see or visualize becomes a part of ourselves.

In many religions, images and meditation are used as ways to identify with and experience a sense of union with the divinity; to experience God as a living force from within, rather than as an external illusion. For instance, in the Yoga Sutras, it is believed that if you focus your attention on a place or an object, you will eventually be able to concentrate so fully that you will be able to blend into the object or achieve union with it, and then you will be able to fully see the truth of that object.

Throughout the history of Western civilization, the literal, linear side has battled with the figurative, metaphorical side for predominance over the way we view life. As we know, ours is a culture in which the word has won over the image. For us, the intuitive, right-hemisphere type of thinking, which perceives through symbols, feelings, images, and poetry, has been subjugated to the rational, language-based processes.

However, in some societies even today the reverse is true. In Bali, for instance, the spiritual world has more significance than the material world. There are cultures all over the world in which the lives of the people are related to their environment in emotional and physical ways, through ceremonies, dances, songs, and drama. In these cultures the people continually experience a connectedness with the universal, the mythical, the visible and invisible realms.

In our culture, we have developed words that enable us to separate ourselves from our environment, until we have become unable to experience nature personally and internally. Rather, we stand back and analyze life for the purpose of manipulating it.

Earlier in history, language (hieroglyphs and ideographs, for example) corresponded to both universal and particular realities. These languages were based on images that were vivid parts of people's lives. Now we use words as tools to categorize experience so we don't have to respond to it.

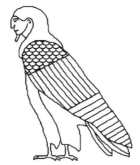

Egyptian symbol for the soul

However, it is still possible for us to learn to see more accurately and to participate more fully in the beauty of the world around us by becoming aware of the details. When we become attentive to the world around us, we can become fully alive and in tune with all life and its potential for happiness and beauty. The details all around us today are the essence of our existence. If we notice the fine points, we can appreciate this moment before it vanishes.

We can retrain ourselves to see the true images of things instead of ignoring them. By noticing the beauty of nature all around us, we live this moment fully, and we can develop a positive point of view as well. Once we have become skilled observers, we can learn to use our inner vision to enrich our lives. This is the point at which mental development transcends words and takes us past the immediate, literal, and material world into the infinite.

When we use words to create a shallow layer of reality to justify our lower motives—our greed for power and control, our pettinesses, lusts, and jealousies—we can never really participate in the true beauty of existence, and we can never truly be alive. So we end up playing Monopoly instead of living.

This symbol reminds us that we can learn to utilize the powers of the beast and transform them into positive energy for life.

Chapter 10
The Hermit

he Hermit holds the lamp of truth. He represents the one who shows the way, illuminating the path for the seekers of the light. He is the source of all personal wisdom and the goal of every endeavor.

Looking at . . .

The Hermit

ou have traveled far and you have seen much. You are walking in the dark, your path covered in shadows. You have taken the withdrawn and the introspective way in search of something that has been hidden.

The Hermit stands among the shadows. He has found inspiration, wisdom, and peace of mind; he has found his soul.

He says to you:

I am _____

I see _____

I have _____

I will _____

I follow _____

The secret message the Hermit tells you is: _____

_____

The Hermit has abandoned the conventions of society to follow his own inner convictions. He is no longer merely a mirror reflecting the influences of outside circumstances. The symbol of the Hermit represents prudence, caution, and restraint in favor of introspection.

The Hermit represents solitude and withdrawal into the self, where there is wisdom and peace.

Say to yourself:
I look inward, seeking the guidance of my higher self as I journey toward deeper understanding and enlightenment.

The following lovely ancient Mandean poem, quoted in Hans Jonas's *The Gnostic Religion*, expresses the symbolism of the Hermit, who looks within for a renewal of life and a conversion of the heart.

The Poem of the Hermit

From the day when we beheld thee,
from the day when we heard thy word, our hearts were filled with peace.
We believed in thee, Good One,
we beheld thy light and shall not forget thee.
All our days we shall not forget thee, not one hour let thee from our hearts,
For our hearts shall not grow blind,
these souls shall not be held back.

From the place of light have I gone forth, from thee, bright habitation . . .
An Uthra who accompanied me from the house of the Great Life
held a staff of living water in his hand.
The staff which he held in his hand
was full of leaves of excellent kind.
He offered me of its leaves,
and prayers and rituals sprang complete from it.
Again he offered me of them
and my sick heart found relief.
A third time he offered me of them,
and he turned upwards the eyes in my head
so that I beheld my Father and knew him.
I beheld my Father and knew him,
and I addressed three requests to him.
I asked him for mildness in which there is no rebellion.
I asked him for a strong heart
to bear both great and small.
I asked him for smooth paths
to ascend and behold the place of light.

In solitude and isolation the Hermit is able to tap the reserves of divine power and insight.

From the day when I came to love the Life,
from the day when my heart came to love the Truth,
I no longer have trust in anything in the world.
In father and mother
I have no trust in the world.
In brothers and sisters
I have no trust in the world . . .
In what is made and created
I have no trust in the world.
In the whole world and its works
I have no trust in the world.
After my soul alone I go searching about,
which to me is worth generations and worlds.
I went and found my soul—
what are to me all the worlds? . . .
I went and found Truth
as she stands at the outer rim of the worlds . . .[8]

There are more than twenty-three symbols in this illustration, including the "Truth as she stands at the outer rim of the worlds."

Looking at . . .

The Lamp

There is a lamp on the road before you. You pick it up. It shines upon the world, lighting everything in a new way.

You see _____

You realize _____

You understand _____

The lamp shows _____

It signifies _____

The lamp is your _____

The lamp represents the light of divinity. It is the symbol of immortality and wisdom. It also stands for guidance, especially divine guidance. The things you see, realize, and feel about the lamp are your responses to wisdom and direction. Your response to the lamp will indicate how you feel in terms of immortality and divine wisdom. Perhaps the lamp holds a message that can give you new insight and understanding.

Looking at . . .

The Cloak

Near the lamp you find a cloak. You put it on and discover that it fits you perfectly. As the cloak envelops you in its deep folds:

You feel _____

You are _____

You can _____

You will _____

The cloak is your _____

Wearing this cloak you can _____

The cloak is a symbol of withdrawal and obscurity. It can symbolize hiding and protection.

How do you feel about the cloak? Through this exercise you may discover the way you feel about withdrawing and hiding. The cloak may seem threatening to you, and you may want to consider the advantages of having time and space for yourself away from the world. Or the cloak may be welcome and feel safe. Do you withdraw a lot? Can you find reasons for feeling that you need to hide?

Looking at . . .   *The Staff*

You find a staff resting against a tree. It is sturdy and you find that it fits your grip.

As you hold the staff in your hand, you realize _____

You feel _____

You understand _____

You have _____

The staff is your _____

With this staff you can _____

You put the staff _____

You decide you will go _____

The staff represents masculine power, authority, dignity, and magical power. It is also a symbol of a journey or a pilgrimage.

What can you learn about your inner feelings regarding power and dignity from your responses to the staff? Do you grasp it easily and eagerly? Or are you reluctant to take it? What are your feelings about your journey or pilgrimage? Will you take up the staff and proceed, or would you rather put it down and turn around?

Looking at . . . *The Cloak, the Staff, and the Lamp*

Now you are wearing the cloak. Your staff is in one hand and your lamp is in the other.

You feel _____

You can _____

You have _____

You will _____

You know _____

You see _____

The lamp, staff, and cloak are the resources of the Hermit, who has withdrawn for inner guidance on his journey.

How do you feel about taking on the characteristics of the Hermit as you look inward for your own inner direction along this pilgrimage to deeper personal understanding? Do you have some negative responses? If so, can you find what has been blocking you? Or are you eager and confident as you proceed along your journey? Do you have new insights to help you understand who you are and why you feel the way you do?

Taking Responsibility

e can always find answers to the problems that confront us in our lives, if we are willing to keep our minds open. First, however, we must operate on the assumption that answers can be found, which implies that there is some kind of meaning and coherence to life.

We are free to believe either that we are born for some purpose, or that we are insignificant. Because we have the choice of what to believe, clearly it is to our advantage to choose to believe that life has meaning and to believe in our own significance. When we assume that life has meaning, our own lives become important; if we assume that something is true we will find the evidence that verifies that assumption.

We make choices every minute of our lives. Even when we are in a circumstance in which we seem to have no choice, we can choose how we will react to that circumstance. Usually, however, we are in a position to make decisions and to take responsibility for the things that happen to us. We are in control of things. We control our actions and our reactions to people and experiences. Naturally, we do not have unlimited choices, but if we accept that fact and adjust our attitudes accordingly, we still remain in control of our reactions.

No matter how strong the forces may be, external conditions cannot determine who and what we will become. We do that ourselves. We decide what we will do, and it is we who must continually choose which way we will go.

Deciding on a Positive Perspective

When something goes wrong we could decide to see it as a sign of our ultimate failure and go no further. In that case, there is no doubt that unhappiness and displeasure would be forthcoming. On the other hand, we can use discouragement as a challenge to motivate us to fight harder, and we can decide to accept nothing less than our goal.

In order to live full lives we have to make positive choices. Outside conditions are undeniably important, but we each have a say about who we are and who we will become. Our attitude toward ourselves teaches others how to treat us.

If we can accept adversity as a natural part of life, we can find the energy to learn from it. When we no longer define hardship as our adversary, but accept it as a natural part of life, it can become a pivotal point in our development. We do not have to interpret adversity as an enemy; instead we can see it as an opportunity to grow.

Just deciding to make the assumption that we are significant and that life is meaningful is a way of taking responsibility for our lives. We are prompted to assess our experiences in an active way when we think of our lives in terms of what we can contribute. This activity itself is stimulating; this is the activity of life, and it brings with it its own satisfactions.

Pleasure and happiness are not passive experiences, and they are not found in retrospect. Usually we think of happiness as something that comes to us when we are waiting for it, but actually pleasure and happiness are active states. In fact, activity brings pleasure, and happiness comes from doing.

The Hermit has searched long and has found his soul, which provides illumination, wisdom, and peace. No longer is he trusting in the material world, now that he has found his own inner light. The message of the Hermit is that you must look within in order to tap the undiscovered self.

The figure of the Hermit represents the strength and autonomy of a person who looks within for approval and guidance and is not influenced by outside circumstances or what other people may think or do. The Hermit carries his own light, from self-understanding. He is cloaked and protected from external vicissitudes, carrying the staff of personal responsibility, inner authority, and self-confidence.

By using his own inner light, the Hermit (with his lamp, cloak, and staff) is able to overcome adversity and find personal satisfaction (represented by the woman).

Looking at . . .

Attitude Assessment

The following exercises can be used to help you clarify in your own mind who you are, where you want to go, and what you want out of life.

Use a separate piece of paper or your journal to list your responses to the following questions.

Assessments

1. What do you like about yourself? List all of your positive attributes.

2. What is good in your life? List everything you have going for you—your job, the place where you live, your friends, family, education, taste, style—anything you feel good about in your life.

3. List your accomplishments. Include any obstacle you have overcome and any victory you have achieved.

4. Make a list of the most important experiences you have had, the peak experiences that have had a pivotal effect on your life.

Goals

1. List all the things you would like to change about yourself.

2. List the things you would like to accomplish.

3. List the most important goals of your life, the things you would like to do, have, and be.

Looking at . . .

Affirmations for Reprogramming Your Attitudes

If you make a decision to change your life, you can do it. Photocopy this page and tape it to your mirror. Repeat each of these sentences to yourself out loud, at least two times a day for thirty days. The message will be heard by your subconscious and take hold, becoming integrated into your life.

1. List the things you like about yourself:

I am _____

2. What is good about your life?

I have _____

3. What have you accomplished?

I have accomplished _____

4. What do you think of as a peak experience of your life, a time when you were at your best?

I remember when I _____

5. What would you like to change about yourself?

I am becoming _____

6. What would you like to change about your life?

My life is becoming more _____

7. What would you like to accomplish in the future?

I am going to _____

8. What are the most important goals of your life?

I will _____

I can _____

Step III in Review

In Step III you have gone through the inward-looking, withdrawal stage of your journey. The Lovers, the Chariot, Strength, and the Hermit have given you tools that will serve you as you proceed along your path. Write down a brief summary of your experience at this portion of your journey.

Write down the most important feeling and insights you have gained from your travels so far.

Step IV
Quest

You have come to a plateau. You were born and initiated, and you have come to a deeper understanding
of yourself and of life. You are now prepared for the
next stage of your journey, in which you must face
challenges and come to terms with your greatest
desires and your deepest fears. The time
has come for you to begin your quest.

Chapter 11
The Wheel of Fortune

he Wheel of Fortune turns throughout time; all of life is in a state of constant change. The Wheel of Fortune indicates to us that life is not a riddle to solve or a goal to reach, but rather it is a constantly changing process of mystery and wonder. It represents time as an endless round of the ever-changing cycles of life.

Wheel of Fortune

ou have left the place of the Hermit, continuing your journey. This is the start of your quest. You have traveled many miles without incident, when gradually the landscape changes and you realize you are venturing into unknown lands. The sky is overcast and the clouds are thick as fog as you move forward. Your path is no longer clear. You pause to decide which way to go, when suddenly out of the clouds an enormous circle appears that looks like an eight-spoked wheel. A sphinx sits at the top of the wheel, and you can see four other figures around it—an angel, an eagle, a lion, and an ox.

The sphinx that sits on top of the wheel says to you:

You are _____

You will _____

You can _____

If you want _____

you must _____

_____

There is a creature at the center of the wheel, who says: _____

The wheel represents the changes of life and the challenge of adapting to change.

At the center of the wheel the hub remains stable. The true self at the center does not move, but rather it causes the wheel to turn. The rim of the wheel revolves, bringing constant change. Both the rim and the hub are parts of the same wheel, each with its own place and function.

The Wheel of Fortune reveals a force within that transcends the apparently random changes in life. When we learn to live in harmony with the center, or the innermost self, we can have control over the direction of the wheel of our lives.

Say to yourself:
The cycles of my life expose me to the conditions I need to experience
to enable me to reach my fullest potential. I focus inward.
From my center I can direct the motion of my life.

Looking at . . .

The Wheel

magine you have come upon an old wheel.

What color is the wheel? _____

Where did it come from? _____

Where did it travel to? _____

What was it used for? _____

How do you feel about it? _____

The wheel represents the changes of life. When we
learn to live in harmony with the center we can
have control of the direction of the wheel.

The wheel represents the cycle of life. Your responses to the questions in
this exercise indicate your feelings about the cycles of change in your own
life.

Looking at . . .

The Two Creatures

 magine you are walking along when suddenly a creature emerges from your head.

What does this creature look like? _____

How do you feel about it? _____

What does it say? _____

Then, a creature emerges from your stomach.

What does this creature look like? _____

How do you feel about it? _____

What does it say? _____

The two creatures meet up with each other. What happens? _____

What do they say to each other?

The creature from your head says: _____

The creature from your stomach says: _____

The creature from your head represents your rational self. The creature from your stomach represents your gut responses, your feelings and instincts. The way these two creatures get along indicates how these two parts of yourself interact. Is one side dominant? Is there violence between them? If so, this indicates that your two processes do not function harmoniously together. In this case, you may want to consider whether your enemy is actually a part of yourself.

Spend some time working to get the two parts into balance, by having the two creatures hold a dialogue in order to come to an agreement. If one side is much stronger than the other, you might give the weak side some extra resources, such as new strengths or weapons. Sit quietly and visualize your two parts in a state of balance and harmony.

Looking at . . . *The Dialogue of the Two Sides*

This exercise will help you gain perspective and understanding when you are confused about your feelings. You may need extra paper or your journal to answer these questions fully.

Think about an important situation that faces you right now, or one that has been bothering you lately. Imagine the issue as two opposing sides that are at odds.

1. Write down the two sides of the issue._____

_____

2. Imagine you are looking into a mirror. The reflection represents one side of the issue; you represent the other. First let the reflection state its position. Then allow the other side, the *you* side, to speak._____

_____

3. Continue this dialogue between the two sides until the whole situation is discussed and you feel you understand the conflicting forces within yourself.

_____

_____

4. Now imagine that the two sides come to an agreement, a compromise, or a mutual understanding. Write it down._____

_____

Think about this solution and how it can help you deal more effectively with your situation.

Born Lucky

father once called his three sons together. He gave the first son a rooster, the second son a scythe, and the third a cat. He said to them, "I am an old man and haven't long to live. As you know, I have no money, but I want to provide something for you before I die, so I have given these things to you. Use them wisely. If you take them to a country where such things are still unknown, your fortune will be made."

After the father died, the eldest son set out with his rooster, but wherever he went, roosters were already known. Finally he came to an island where roosters were still unknown, and where the people didn't even know how to tell time. The boy told the islanders how his bird would crow three times in the night at regular intervals, the last time just before sunrise. The people were delighted with the rooster and paid the young man a fortune for it.

The second son, seeing how successful his brother had been, set out with his scythe, looking for a far-off place where the people had never seen one before. He reached a distant island where it was time to harvest the grain from the fields, so he showed the people how to use his scythe. They were so grateful to have the scythe that they paid him a fortune for it.

The third son set out with his cat. After traveling to a very far-off country, he finally found a town that had no cats and was overridden with mice. The cat set to work at once in the king's palace hunting mice. The people were so delighted they paid the boy a fortune for the cat.

The cat killed all the mice in the palace. Then it became thirsty and said, "Meow." This frightened the king and his courtiers, so they ran out of the palace. Outside they decided to send the cat a message, telling it to leave the palace at once. The cat's response was, "Meow."

The king took this to be a negative reply, and he had his palace bombarded by the town cannon. The palace went up in flames. The cat jumped out the window, but the king's men kept bombarding the palace until it was leveled to the ground.

This story is an illustration of the idea that we can either turn situations that seem hopeless into opportunities, or we can fail to take advantage of opportunities, depending on our attitudes. Life goes on all around us, but the person who keeps a steady inner perspective can turn any situation into an advantage.

The three sons in this story were able to find their fortunes by using their imaginations. The king caused his own ruination because he expected and assumed the worst. He made no inquiries and did not ask for help. Instead of finding a resource and taking advantage of it, the king ignorantly assumed that the unknown was hostile. As a result he destroyed his own castle needlessly.

Often we interpret a situation negatively, or respond in needlessly destructive ways, creating disaster for ourselves as a consequence. On the other hand, something of ours that we consider ordinary (like the cat or rooster in the story) can become a great advantage to us, if we find the right place to use it.

The figures on the wheel above are doomed to rise and fall with the changes in their fortunes, but the person who learns to stay at the center remains stable and balanced.

The symbol of the wheel reminds us that if we keep our focus centered on the hub, we can avoid self-destructive attitudes and find ways to use our gifts to our best advantage, instead of spinning around aimlessly through the ups and downs of life.

Reflections . . .

The Wheel

ll things change. The cycle of existence runs externally through our lives. We know both darkness and light, strength and weakness, joy and sorrow, life and death. We are carried along with the perpetual motion of life. If we are governed by change, we will be forever unstable and insecure, one moment knowing success and feeling jubilant, the next moment knowing misfortune and feeling devastated. The Wheel of Fortune teaches us that if we can become detached from the ongoing cycle, we can take control of our own destinies.

At the center of the wheel is the soul, the point of light around which the whole world and the universe turn. In ancient mythology, the wheel of the world and the wheel of God's spheres are united on an axis through which the sun shines and circulates the energy of material and divine existence. This is where the tree of life grows, joining the earthly with the divine.

Existence begins at every moment. Around each here rolls there.
The middle is everywhere. The way of eternity is a curve.

P. D. Ouspensky

Often we see ourselves as victims of the incessant turnings of the wheel, which will bring us hardship or glory, and we have no power or control over it. However, when we can remove ourselves from the cycle by using the faculties of the imagination and the powers of faith, we can find stability in the changing cosmos, and we can learn to gain control of our destinies. When we are in charge of our own lives, we can find advantages where none had been apparent before.

A Focus on Growth

**W**hen we take the negative and turn it into energy for productivity, we can transform our worst situations into positive, beneficial ones. Understanding that there is always the possibility for growth can change our attitudes toward life's experiences. This approach by itself can make the difference between happiness and unhappiness.

Research has proven over and over that a person's attitude dramatically affects the outcome of a situation. If you expect the worst, you will get it. If you look for the best, you can find it. The lesson is that if you change your attitude toward yourself and your situation, your life will automatically become changed.

The external world of our reality—the daily newspaper headline interpretation of existence—is often replete with negative messages. These outward negative messages feed our own inner insecurities and fears, and we find ourselves trapped in a cloud of anxieties and pressures. Furthermore, when we see ourselves in outward terms we can never be satisfied. We can never be skinny enough, rich enough, or successful enough. In fact, as measured by the outside world, we can never be good enough. Someone is always ahead of us in one way or another, if we measure ourselves by their appearance.

It is only when we learn to evaluate ourselves in terms of our own inner values that we can exist in a positive emotional state, aware of the continual opportunities for growth and for feelings of satisfaction.

Often when we experience tension we try to find ways to cover it up or to repress it. We may pretend we no longer remember what it was that bothered us. Then we discover that we have a skin condition, an ulcer, bad digestion, a twitch, or some other little ailment. If we deny the underlying problem long enough, we find ourselves in the middle of a life crisis. This is because denying problems always backfires. We cannot rid ourselves of our problems by repressing them.

If we try to get around a problem by blaming someone else or some extenuating circumstance, we render ourselves powerless to change the problem.

On the other hand, when we face a tension-causing situation and work it out positively and creatively instead of attempting to avoid it, we can change the toxic effects of the experience of stress into new forms of energy. Therefore, it is beneficial to face adversity instead of denying it or trying to escape it. It will not damage us to face our problems. We will actually profit from dealing with adversity, because we will be able to find solutions. In addition, the act of facing up to our challenges itself will give us renewed energy, enthusiasm, and zest for life.

Much does he gain who, when he loses, learns.
Michelangelo

Not all tension and stress is bad; it depends on how you interpret it. The glass can be half-empty or half-full.

If life were entirely stress-free, we wouldn't be alive and growing. The body and mind would atrophy if they did not experience some tension. Excess stress and anxiety must, of course, be dealt with in order for us to maintain good health. But happiness and mental well-being are not produced by a lack of tension; rather they come from dealing effectively with the problems that cause tension and knowing how to counterbalance them with positive conditioning techniques.

Everyone's life is filled with difficulties and challenges, but we can learn from the pain. When we figure out where a problem fits on the cycle of our life's journey we can chart our course accordingly, and every experience will become simply another part of the greater pattern of life.

If we learn to become detached from the outer shell of ego defenses, we can accept and even love ourselves and our circumstances. It is at this point that we will be released from the cycles of the Wheel of Fortune, to take control of our lives.

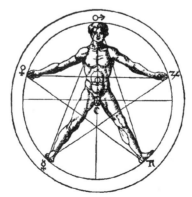

When we learn to accept adversity, we can be released from the cycles of fortune.

Chapter 12
Justice

he symbol of Justice represents the faculty of discrimination, which gives us perspective and judgment and enables us to make sense of the events that occur in our lives, in order to determine our values and establish our priorities. This is the symbol of inner self-direction.

Looking at . . .

The Figure of Justice

 long the straight and narrow path you have been traveling, you see a great hall up ahead. As you approach the entrance, you see a woman sitting on a throne, holding a sword in her right hand and a scale in her left hand. You note a sense of order, harmony, and balance as you gaze into the large room where she is sitting. The room is light and quiet and very cool. The Justice figure sits very still, and you can sense her inner calm and balance.

She says to you:

My greatest law is _____

I will give you my sword for _____

The scales I give to you for _____

The just and proper outcome will occur if you simply _____

_____

The guidance from the figure of Justice will tell you what is needed in a situation you are facing.

As we have already seen, the sword represents power and authority. In this context, it also represents justice and the power of discrimination. Over what will the sword give you power of judgment and discrimination?

The scales of Justice represent balance, fairness, and harmony. In what way will they be of use to you, based on your response in this exercise? What must you do in order to find the just and proper outcome at this juncture in your life?

Say to yourself:
I am able to distinguish clearly the true from the false. I take charge
of my life and I face the issues in my life with honesty.

Looking at . . .

The Sword and the Scales

You hold the sword in your right hand and the scales in your left hand.

You are _____

You have _____

You will _____

You feel _____

Your quest is for _____

_____

You possess the powers of discrimination from the sword, and inner harmony and balance from the scales. In what aspect of your life can you best utilize these gifts?

Looking at . . .

Two Animals

1. Put yourself into a quiet, relaxed, and peaceful state of mind.

2. Picture in your mind a beautiful outdoor scene. Listen to the sounds and enjoy the sights of nature all around you. Feel the fresh air and smell the fragrances. See all the colors and the textures of the day.

3. Imagine you are approached by an animal that symbolizes one side of a problem or an issue that has been bothering you. Try to see the animal in detail, noticing its color, shape, and size.

4. Imagine there is another animal, one that represents the other side of your problem.

5. The two animals meet. There is a confrontation and the creatures battle. Watch the fight as it progresses in your imagination. After the battle is over, you will understand why you do what you do and you will know which side of yourself is stronger than the other.

6. If you want to change the balance of power, give the weaker side some powers or weapons to allow it to win the battle.

When you can imagine the conflict between the two sides of a problem and see which side holds the most power, you will be able to understand the forces that motivate you and learn to alter them, if necessary.

The Story of the Miser

here was once a miser who sold everything he had and melted down his hoard of gold into a single lump, which he then buried in a field. Every day he went to look at the spot where his gold was buried. Sometimes he would spend long hours gloating over his treasure.

One day his servant noticed the master's frequent visits to the hiding place. He followed him and discovered the miser's secret. Then, in the dark of night when nobody was around, the servant dug up all the miser's gold and ran away.

The next day the miser visited his hiding place and discovered that his treasure had been stolen. He cried and screamed out in his agony, howling so loudly that his neighbor heard him and rushed over to find out what was the matter.

The neighbor asked the miser what had upset him so. The miser explained that all his worldly goods had been buried and that his life's joy had been to visit the place where they were buried, where he would sit and gaze at the spot for hours.

The wise neighbor said to the miser, "Don't take this loss so hard, my friend. All you have to do is put a brick into the hole where the gold was buried and visit it every day. You will be no worse off than before when your gold was buried and of no earthly good to you."

It is said that we get out of life what we put into it. If we hold ourselves back from life, we end up with nothing, like the miser whose only joy was to look at the place where his money was buried. When we overcome external illusions and distractions, we gain an inner emotional strength that gives us psychological power, so that we can deal with life with wisdom and understanding.

The symbol of Justice depicts the obligation each of us has to assume responsibility over our lives and to overcome superstitious ideas and vain illusions through positive self-direction. The figure of Justice represents the ability to discriminate in order to develop appropriate values and priorities.

Reflections . . .

The Importance of Goals

he figure of Justice also represents the capacities both for mercy and for clear, impartial judgment. When we have tasks to perform and goals to reach, life becomes active and interesting. Having goals gives life a sense of motion and growth. Through this sense of motion and growth we will be able to achieve contentment.

The purpose of life is not to be happy. The purpose of life is to matter, to be productive, to have it make some difference that you live at all. Happiness, in the ancient noble verse, means self-fulfillment and is given to those who use to the fullest whatever talents God or luck bestowed upon them.

Leo Rosten

Weighing the true importance of things over their material value will provide us with a sense of beauty and profound meaning.

The Balance of Life

ontentment will result from understanding and judging the experiences of life wisely. If we expect all things to go our way, we will be disappointed. But if we are lonely, we can always decide to give a party; if we want to work, we can offer our services.

By accepting ourselves with all our limitations and failures, we become able to love and be loved by others. When we feel secure within, accepting and loving ourselves, we are no longer empty shells waiting for something outside to come and save us from our desperate states of lovelessness and loneliness. When our attitude toward life is loving, we are free to experience a loving exchange with the world.

By adopting an attitude of giving, looking for the needs of others to serve, we can eliminate the painful ego blows that create much of our unhappiness. We know that if we wait for someone else to give us happiness we are sure to be disappointed, for happiness can only come from within. And happiness comes most easily when we are participating rather than waiting to take from life.

The highest destiny of the individual is to serve rather than to rule
or to impose himself in any other way.

Albert Einstein

By using our powers of discrimination we can develop a sense of purpose and of significance to give life boundaries and direction. Wisely judging what is really important and true for us will provide us with a sense of beauty and of profound meaning, whether it comes from art, music, or some kind of spiritual development. This is the kind of experience that cannot be explained or measured by mechanical or material means; its truth and value are not only intrinsic but also priceless.

Happiness

ost of us seek happiness throughout our lives, and most of us have come to believe that it is an illusory concept. We may spend a lot of time looking for it, but we are never quite sure what it is. People say that money can't buy happiness. Where does happiness come from? Obviously what brings one person happiness will not create that same response in the next person. This is because happiness comes from within, not from external sources.

Happiness can be found in the same place as our sense of spirituality and our creativity, imagination, inspiration, and insights. It is part of the life of the inner self. It is an outlook, not based on any tangible goals or material things; it is simply a way of feeling. We may associate a new car, a new job, or the admiration, respect, and envy of others with the idea of happiness, but since those things come from outside and happiness comes from within, they are actually not related. A momentary thrill of flattery or the acquisition of some desired object may give us a feeling of happiness for a short time, but even the most wealthy, brilliant, and admired person does not necessarily feel fulfilled by these external experiences.

When people are happy they have more successes than when they are unhappy, because people respond in a positive way to someone who is cheerful. According to studies, happy people are more healthy than unhappy people. When people are happy, their perceptions are sharper; they have better senses of smell, hearing, and vision than when they are unhappy. Even memory works better when people are happy.

Happy people usually laugh easily. Studies have indicated that laughing is one of nature's best antidotes for illness. The physical act of laughing causes an increase in the body's oxygen supply, and the diaphragm massages the heart. Blood pressure drops and anxieties fade when we are able to laugh.

However, most of us have developed the idea that happiness is something we earn only if we are good enough, as if happiness were a privilege one achieves by being hard-working and successful. But happiness is not a quantitative, logical experience. It does not fit into a cause-and-effect equation. It is not a moral issue, it is a state of mind. Happiness is not the reward we earn for good behavior, it is virtue in itself.

It has been suggested that the state of happiness produces goodness, that a happy person behaves more kindly than an unhappy one. If we observe ourselves we can undoubtedly find examples of our inner state of unhappiness causing us to behave unkindly or, on the other hand, our happiness inspiring an attitude of goodwill toward others.

Attitudes

f happiness is not to be earned or gained through virtuous acts, how can we find it? Where does it come from? The answer is that we can be happy simply by cultivating a cheerful, positive attitude. That doesn't mean we will have no problems, but we can learn to accept our problems as a natural part of life's process. Having problems is inevitable; everyone always has them. Sometimes these upsets are minor and sometimes they are enormous, but they are a fact of life. No state of life is problem-free.

Once we accept our difficulties as inevitable, we can get rid of the resentment we felt over having them. Then we are free to work on their solutions with a positive attitude and even to begin to enjoy the challenge of solving them. Solving a problem will give us a sense of personal satisfaction that in itself will produce a feeling of happiness.

Most people are about as happy as they make up their minds to be.
Abraham Lincoln

We can spend our whole lives waiting for that future experience that will bring us great happiness. Then we reach the top of the hill and discover that happiness is over the next one, and then the next one—the one we can never reach.

The Symbols of Justice

The sword is for cutting away ignorance, self-pity, and all other vain delusions about how life is supposed to be. This gives us a clearer vision of ourselves and our lives, so that we can distinguish what is important from what is not. Thus we can evaluate our actions and responses in terms of our ideals and our goals.

The scales represent our capacity to weigh experiences as we find them, clearly understanding their place in the scheme of things. They also remind us of our capacity to balance our responses to them.

This illustration shows Roger Bacon, a thirteenth-century English monk and philosopher, holding the scales, which are, with the sword, the symbols of the image of Justice.

Step IV in Review

In Step IV you encountered the Wheel of Fortune and Justice. They help you define the issues in your life that constitute the basic purpose for your journey. Write down a brief summary of what you feel is the essential nature of your quest.

Write down the most important feeling and insights you have gained about your pilgrimage to self-development.

Step V
Into the Realms of Death

You must now prepare to enter the realms of death.
You have found the resources you will need
to pass through these regions.

Quiet your mind and open your heart, for this is the
passage through the netherworld. You will be asked
to give up much. This is the only way to travel
safely when you come into these lands.

Chapter 13
The Hanged Man

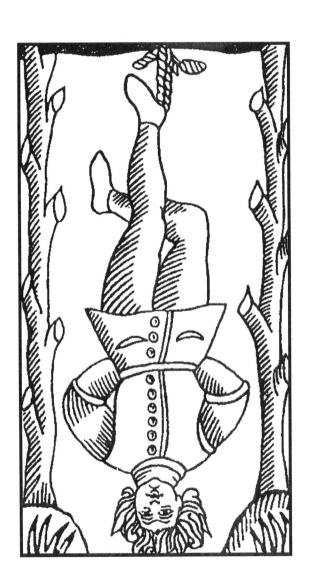

his symbol of the Hanged Man represents a voluntary death to some aspect of the known world, in an act of faith, so that a new and important aspect of the psyche may be recovered that will enable us to live richer and more fulfilled lives.

THE HANGED MAN.

Looking at . . .

The Hanged Man

 ou are walking through the woods. There is a chill in the air and you have a vague feeling of apprehension, but you travel forward in spite of your misgivings. At the top of a gentle hill you see a man who is suspended by his foot from the Tree of Life.

He speaks to you. He says:

In an act of faith, you must give up your _____

The lesson you must learn is _____

The only way to do this is by _____

The rewards for your sacrifice will be _____

which will enable you to _____

Then he tells you:

I am the _____

I have _____

My destiny is _____

The Hanged Man represents sacrifice, especially the sacrifice of the visible for a transcendent good. This may mean giving up old attitudes and beliefs, or it may represent giving up the security of the known, material world in order to explore the underworld of the psyche.

What are the things you must give up, and what will the rewards be if you do?

Sacrifice is a submitting to divine guidance through reconciliation, offering the self to the will of God.

Say to yourself:
I give up all my old attachments, prejudices, and fears. I give up all that inhibits my growth. I have faith that my sacrifice of the limitations of the known will lead me to new and bountiful rewards and fulfillment.

The Myth of Prometheus

In some versions of Greek mythology, the god Prometheus was the creator of humankind. It was he who, using earth and water and his own tears, fashioned the body of the first man, into which the goddess Athena breathed soul and life.

But the great god Zeus required mankind to make a sacrifice to him of their oxen. A meeting was held to decide which portion of the ox should go to man and which to Zeus. Prometheus decided to fool Zeus into choosing the larger portion, which was just fat and bone, leaving the meat to mankind. But Zeus saw the trick and flew into a rage. In his anger, he withheld fire from the human race.

Prometheus stole a branch of holy fire.

Prometheus, however, went to the island of Lemnos and stole a branch of holy fire. He enclosed it in a hollow stalk and carried it back to humankind. Prometheus was made to pay cruelly for this deception and theft. Zeus had him chained to a crest in the Caucasus Mountains. There, an eagle with outstretched wings, sent by Zeus, fed upon his immortal liver. As much as the winged monster devoured during the day, that much grew again during the night.

Finally, after thirty years of suffering, Zeus permitted Cheron, who had been struck with a poisoned arrow, to take Prometheus' place and Prometheus was set free.

The theme of sacrifice represents the concept that adversity is the only way to achieve growth. The idea is that giving up personal gain or even life itself is the vehicle to a greater good than one's own self-interest.

He who loves this life shall lose it, and he who hates his life
in this world will keep it for eternal life.

John 12:25

Sacrifice

 theme that appears in many cultures with great frequency is that of creation taking place only after a living being has been sacrificed. This holds true for all levels of existence. Mircea Eliade says, "The mythic pattern remains the same: nothing can be created without immolation, without sacrifice."[9]

Numerous mythic figures made this kind of sacrifice, abandoning their known worlds to go down into the underworld in order to reclaim a lost treasure. Hercules, Odysseus, Theseus, and Orpheus were some of the Greek mythic figures who sacrificed their known worlds to go off on a quest.

The two sides, the dark and the light, are shown in a relationship in which each sacrifices in order to attain a synthesis that provides a wholeness greater than the sum of its parts.

To sacrifice is to voluntarily give up something in order to gain something else of greater value. In the old print above, we see an example of sacrifice; in this case the ego is sacrificed to the marriage relationship.

The Hanged Man represents the hero who must undergo trials in order to truly become a hero. Ultimately this will lead to the greatest of all trials, in which we ourselves, as the hero, must give up thinking in terms of our own egos and come to a transcendent state of consciousness.

Carl Jung said, "Our unconscious always puts us into impossible situations in order to bring out our best." An impossible situation in which we must renounce our own will and rely on our trust and faith brings about personal growth.

Our identity is composed of our assessment of ourselves based on the sum of our life experiences. We are limited by the boundaries of what we know and what we believe. We are cut off from potential development in new areas by our lack of experience. Thus we often cling to negative and self-limiting views of ourselves out of habit. Ironically, this habit can be broken only by the conditions of duress and hardship that produce anxiety. The discomfort of anxiety can force us to break down old habits, allowing our identities to change and grow.

By understanding the necessity for the trials of life, we can learn to appreciate them, which makes them easier for us to overcome. When we are so afraid of difficulties that we live our lives trying to dodge them, we stunt ourselves as well as suffering needlessly from the troubles that finally catch up with us.

According to Freud, nothing is an accident. If you stub your toe, you should look for the message the incident has for you. By learning to communicate with our inner selves, we can gain control over the accidents in our lives. If we experience illness and adversity, the experience often turns out to be a great instrument for our personal growth, a response to things we have refused or been unable to deal with consciously. If we have unconsciously participated in the creation of our own illness, we can learn to listen to our inner needs before they go so far as to become manifested as physical ailments.

We can avoid a great deal of susceptibility to disease by our attitude toward illness. The human body is (as in the myth of Prometheus) a wonderful organism constantly seeking to rejuvenate itself. The body's natural condition is to be healthy, energetic, and vital.

Medicine and the Mind

ore and more medical professionals are beginning to realize that health is a reflection of inner harmony on a psychological and spiritual as well as a physical level. The causes of ill health are often based not only on factors outside ourselves, but on our attitudes and behavior as well. What we think and do influences the way we feel.

We know that the mind can, if properly motivated, cause the production of pain-killing agents even when no drugs have been administered. This placebo effect is an example of how faith and mental attitude can be critical factors in the body's healing.

The cells that cause cancer in the body are always present. It is only when we are under too much stress that the body is unable to fight off the cancer cells.

When we suppress anger, a chemical action causes the secretion of acids that can attack parts of the body, as in the case of ulcers. Anger, tension, stress, and anxiety affect the heart and circulation, which in turn affect other parts of the body. In fact, some physicians say that mental control of the body, or psychosomatic conditions, may account for over 80 percent of all illness.

Scientists have discovered that an experience that is a "pain in the neck" may end up as a physical neck ache. A rigid frame of mind may become expressed as arthritis. A broken heart may be manifested by a coronary, and a need for growth can show up as cancer.

Clearly, we need to learn how to control our thinking in order to control our health. We need to learn how to respond positively to life's dilemmas in order to avoid the dangers produced by stress, tension, and other negative attitudes and habits.

Sometimes when we are faced with a stressful situation we respond by having a cigarette, a cup of coffee, a drink, a pill, or a candy bar. Unfortunately, ingestion of these chemicals increases the stresses on the body even further. However, we can learn to control or eliminate these dangerous stress-causing chemicals, and reduce the strain on our bodies.

The eagle represents personal strength and victory.

Each of us is capable of tremendous control over our own physical health. Under hypnosis, patients have been able to diagnose their own illnesses when doctors have been baffled. The body can understand and heal itself more than we realize.

By learning to relax the body and to view situations positively instead of dwelling on the negative aspects of life, we can free our bodies of the extra tensions and stress that produce illness. If we focus on the positive aspects of life, we can improve our health as well as our frame of mind, because the unconscious mind will take our messages of mental well-being and convert them into physical and mental health.

Inside the egg, the divine child, the symbol of a new attitude of harmony and self-acceptance, is produced as a result of the union of the opposites (the conscious and the unconscious). He stands on the sun and the moon. The birds signify the spiritual aspect of this kind of emotional rebirth, and the rays of the sun represent the importance of emotion.

The Mind and the Body

he mind and the body are one inseparable system. Everything we think and feel is expressed in the body. What we believe and the ways we view life have direct effects on our health. Therefore, if we change the things we believe, we will change the way we feel.

Thus we can take an active, positive, and responsible role in healing ourselves by becoming more aware of how we feel. One way we can do this is to learn to communicate with our unconscious, the point of origin for our feelings.

Occasionally, it takes disease to teach us the laws of health, just as friction in human relationships can lead us to discover the ways of harmony. Everything that happens in our lives can serve to lead us to health, happiness, peace, and wisdom if we are able to learn the lessons of our experiences.

Having a positive outlook is a habit. Nobody can hurt us unless we allow it, and if we are relaxed and confident we will not allow it. Unhappiness is also a habit, and we can avoid it through a change in attitude. When you are feeling anxious and unhappy, call to mind pleasant ideas, dreams, and memories. You can use your will to alter your thoughts. If you think about peaceful ideas, you will feel calm and relaxed, and your mind will open to the inspirations that bring solutions to your problems.

The obstacles that keep us from mental and physical well-being are based on a preoccupation with ourselves. If we feel we are less than perfect, we don't want to risk failure by making mistakes. This is why we cannot live life to the fullest until we feel confident and secure within. It is important for us to recognize that our accomplishments are not based on anybody else's assessment of our abilities; what matters is what we think of ourselves, and much of that comes from past programs we have run like tape recordings in our minds, until they have become habitual patterns.

The message of sacrifice is that of giving up old habits and self-limitations, in favor of growth and mental and physical health.

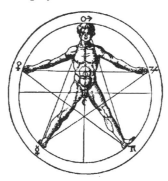

Looking at . . .

How to Counteract Anxiety

1. Sit in a relaxed position in a comfortable chair.

2. Say aloud to yourself, "I have unlimited resources for strength and wisdom from the infinite, and I have the limitless power of my unconscious mind."

3. Breathe slowly and deeply for a few seconds. Then say aloud to yourself, "I have health and strength. I have the ability to meet my highest goals."

4. When you have anxious thoughts and find you are focusing on the negative aspects of a situation, change your thoughts. Think of something positive. When worries interfere with your ability to concentrate, close your eyes for a moment and think about your hopes and dreams. Then positively and aggressively address yourself to the situation at hand.

   If you are unable to function at your best due to anxiety, close your eyes and think about good, successful experiences you have had in the past. Say to yourself, "I can easily attain all the things of which I dream."

5. Remember, to counteract anxiety you must feel good about yourself, and feeling good about yourself is a habit of thinking. If your habit of thinking has been negative, spend some time, at least fifteen minutes twice a day, in a relaxed state, giving yourself positive messages. Say to yourself, "I will reach my goals. All obstacles that face me are opportunities in disguise."

Looking at . . .

Overcoming Bad Memories

1. Sit peacefully in a relaxed state for several minutes.

2. Picture an experience that has been bothering you. See it vividly, in detail. Remember who was there and what happened as clearly as you can.

3. In your mind, enclose the whole scene in a magical balloon.

4. Let the balloon go, and watch as it gently floats up into the sky.

5. Say to the balloon filled with incidents and people from your memory, "I release you." Watch as the balloon floats off into the sky and out of sight.

6. How do you feel?

_____

_____

Looking at . . .

The Golden Ball

1. Quiet your mind. Sit quietly and comfortably, allowing all distracting thoughts to leave your mind until you reach a quiet mental state.

2. Say to yourself, "Everything is in its proper order. There is a harmonious and correct solution to every situation."

3. Visualize a golden ball. Try to actually see it. If you cannot, imagine that you see it. Say to yourself, "I am becoming peacefully aware of the perfect answers for me."

4. Look at the golden ball in your mind. With your mind quiet and open, wait until answers appear to you from within the ball.

Write down what you see in the golden ball.

He rides a white horse; wherever he passes, night will follow. Flowers wither and leaves drop to the ground. All who see him fall to their knees.

The sun sinks here, but as it does so it rises there. Life comes to birth and then dies, and as it dies it comes to birth.

DEATH.

Looking at . . .

Death

he king falls from his throne. All that exists will change. Soon you will have to sail the river to the land beyond the hill, until you reach two pillars.

What happened that led you to this point? _____

_____

How do you feel? _____

Finish these sentences:

This is the end of _____

I miss _____

I understand that _____

I have learned that _____

I accept _____

I will _____

I must _____

I know _____

I release _____

There will be _____

Death to the earthly life must take place before a spiritual rebirth. The symbol of Death stands for the letting go—perhaps just of old habits and patterns, or maybe of a greater loss, in order to make way for a new life. It symbolizes transformation by moving through ordeal to rebirth. The lesson of Death is that we must accept and let go of the past; that rebirth and regeneration are vital parts of life, and they occur only after a great loss.

Your comments indicate your perspective at this juncture, and they reflect your attitude toward the changes you must face and accept in your life.

The symbol of Death represents letting go of something to make way for the new.

Say to yourself:
I am ready for a renewal of myself,
I look forward to a time of spiritual regeneration.

Looking at . . .

The Ship

You see a ship as you are gazing out at sea.

To whom does this ship belong? _____

What is the cargo the ship carries? _____

How do you feel about it? _____

Where is the ship going? _____

The ship symbolizes setting out on the sea of life and crossing the waters of death, or moving from this point in your life to the next. This exercise will give you some understanding of how you feel about change as you find yourself entering the realms of the unknown.

Looking at . . .

Boarding the Great Boat

The great boat is waiting. You hesitate, but you know you must board at once. You climb onto the deck, and the ship sets off for the farthest shore.

You feel _____

You know _____

On this trip you hope to find _____

The purpose of this journey is to _____

The Farthest Shore

Finally the ship reaches the farthest shore, to leave you in the land beyond the hills, past the two pillars—the terrible land of the Great Beyond.

You have come here because _____

You feel _____

You must _____

Your task is to _____

You can _____

The Return Home

Finally the great boat returns for you. You are now ready to go back home.

You understand _____

You feel _____

You have become _____

You will _____

As in the earlier exercise of the ship, boarding the great boat symbolizes setting out on the sea of life and crossing the waters of death, or changing from this point in life to the next. This exercise asks you to express your feelings about this journey and its purpose for you.

In the second exercise, the farthest shore represents your arrival at the "terrible land of the Great Beyond," or your own inner depths. This land beyond the hills represents your entry into a new life, or a new mode of living.

In the third exercise, the return home represents your return to the daylight world. Your answers indicate what you have learned and what you will bring back within yourself from your journey.

The purpose of this voyage is for rebirth and regeneration. Change is inevitable and important. The challenge is to accept change and to discover tomorrow, as we rediscover ourselves. These exercises will give you a glimpse of the nature and direction of your journey. Your responses indicate what you need to accept and to accomplish, and what you can gain from the losses and changes in your life.

We looked briefly at the myth of Demeter and Persephone in chapter 4. Here we look at it again in greater detail.

The Myth of Persephone

ccording to ancient Greek mythology, Demeter, the great goddess of corn and grain, the mother goddess, had one daughter, Persephone. Persephone was beautiful and cheerful and loved her mother very much. Mother and daughter could often be seen wandering arm in arm across the meadows, laughing and dancing. Persephone and her friends loved to take long walks, picking the most beautiful spring flowers Demeter had created.

Demeter warned Persephone of the dangers of the black night if she should wander off too far. She told her lovely daughter to be careful always to return home before nightfall.

One day the young goddess and her friends had wandered far in search of a brilliant red flower. They danced and sang and wove wreaths in one another's hair until late in the day. The golden light of the sun began to fade into dusk and the girls were far from home. Suddenly there was a loud noise and the earth began to tremble. Persephone looked up from the wreath she had been weaving to see a stark white stallion whose rider was dressed in a flowing cape as black as midnight. The horse swept by and in an instant the rider leaned over and captured the terrified Persephone. In that instant the meadows and hillsides vanished, and all Persephone could see was a long black tunnel.

Persephone's friends ran back to Demeter and told her what they had seen. Demeter did not hesitate but went at once to the great god Zeus, the king of thunder and the ruler of gods and men. "The king of the underworld has stolen my beautiful daughter," Demeter said. "You must order him to return her to the light of day at once!" Zeus replied, "Demeter, you know that the lord of Hades is rich and powerful. He owns all the gold and silver, the emeralds and rubies and diamonds in his kingdom, the underworld.

"As the ruler of all the gods, I can command him and he must obey, but I can only get your child back if she has nothing to eat while she is in the underworld. If Persephone accepts one morsel of food or drink from Hades, lord of the underworld, then she must remain with him."

Down in the dark depths of the earth, Hades ordered a magnificent banquet prepared for the young goddess. Platter after platter of sumptuous meats and breads were set before Persephone. Rare and delicate vegetables and delectable  dishes from all over the world were brought to tempt her, but Persephone only shook her head and refused to eat. Wonderful fruits were offered to her, each the most magnificent of its kind—apples, grapes, oranges, bananas, ripe berries of every kind, peaches, pears, and mangoes. On the top of one large platter was a beautiful ripe pomegranate.

By this time Persephone was very tired and thirsty. She had been in the underworld a long time and had eaten nothing. She took the pomegranate and raised it to her lips. As she swallowed the first mouthful, Hades boomed for all the earth and all the gods on Mount Olympus to hear, "Persephone has eaten six seeds of the pomegranate. For each of these seeds, she must stay with me in the underworld for one month each year."

The great god Zeus agreed that Persephone must stay with Hades in the underworld for six months of each year because she had eaten six seeds of the magic pomegranate. Demeter, in her rage and sorrow over her lost daughter, wandered all over the earth. Everywhere she went the flowers died and the trees became bare. She covered the land in ice and snow and refused to allow anything to grow as long as her daughter was in the underworld.

After four bleak and cold months, Demeter went to the underworld to demand the return of her daughter. At first Hades refused to let Persephone go, but Zeus knew there would be no crops until Demeter was satisfied, so he ordered Hades to free the young goddess.

The mother and daughter returned joyfully to the earth and at once spring reappeared. Flowers began to bloom and green leaves sprouted on the trees. The grain and corn, grapes and apples began to grow again. For six months the two goddesses celebrated the bounty of the earth.

But once again winter returned when Persephone went back to the underworld. All the earth mourned for her, and her mother refused to let the crops grow. And to this day the cycle of summer and winter reminds us of the loss of the goddess Persephone and the sorrow of her mother.

The story of Orpheus and Eurydice is one of many classic tales of death and resurrection. This tale, and hundreds of similar stories throughout the world, tells of the possibility of a return of the lover with his lost love from the netherworld. But some little fault or slight frailty makes this reunion finally impossible.

Orpheus and Eurydice

ost of the earliest musicians were gods, but a few mortals performed so well that they were nearly as good as the gods. By far the greatest of these was Orpheus. When he played or sang, no one could resist him. Everything animate and inanimate followed him.

Eurydice was the beloved bride of Orpheus. One day soon after their wedding, she was bitten by a snake as she walked along the river bank. The snake's venom quickly killed her.

In his grief, Orpheus went to Persephone to ask her how to get Eurydice back. Persephone told Orpheus that he could get into the underworld to rescue his wife by charming its inhabitants with his music. She warned Orpheus that once he found Eurydice, he must not look back at her until they reached the upper world.

Following Persephone's advice, Orpheus sang of his bride on his lyre. Then he went down into the underworld to find her, singing as he went. His singing held all of Hades spellbound. Death's very home was shaken to hear the beauty of his song. Even the Furies and the three-mouthed Cerberus were lulled. Ixion's wheel ceased to turn. Taking advantage of this lull, Orpheus found his wife and quickly began to retrace his steps back toward the upper world, followed by Eurydice.

The two passed through the great doors of Hades to the path that would lead them out of the darkness. Orpheus knew that Eurydice followed him, but he desperately wanted to look behind to be sure. When he had nearly reached the daylight, Orpheus turned to her, but it was too soon. She was still in the cavern. He held out his arms to reach her, but in that instant she was gone. She had slipped back into the darkness.

Orpheus tried to rush down after her, but he was not permitted to enter the underworld a second time while he still lived.

Reflections . . .

The Journey into Darkness

he hero ventures out of the land he knows, into darkness. There he accomplishes his adventure. As he prepares to reemerge safely into the world of awakened consciousness, he commits a fatal error. He attempts to merge the two worlds, but the rules of one world do not apply to the other. He looks back—or Persephone eats one small piece of the forbidden fruit from the underworld.

When the conscious mind attempts to control or manipulate the unconscious realm, the whole regeneration process is lost. The two realms cannot be joined. Feelings and instincts demand complete fidelity. Their realm will not be contaminated or manipulated by technology or materialism. To attempt to do so is fatal for the psyche.

Perhaps this is why we see so many architectural monstrosities. This may also explain writer's block, when the writer tries to force a work instead of letting it flow out from his creative subconscious mind, or the realms of the underworld.

On the other hand, we must descend into the darkness of the underworld before rising to eternal clarity. Without sin there can be no salvation. Without death there is no resurrection.

That which thou sowest is not quickened, except it die.

Paul, 1 Cor. 15:36

The symbol of Death speaks to us of the inescapable necessity for each of us to go down into the underworld in order to become transformed, whether the issue at hand is to grow from a child to an adult, to create a masterpiece, or simply to find a renewed sense of meaning and peace of mind. But we are warned that we must take this journey as we find it, with no hidden expectations or manipulative purposes. The journey to the underworld will name its own terms, and we must comply with them absolutely, or the whole purpose of the venture will be lost to us.

The image of Death is also the image of new beginnings.

The Symbol of Death

*Truly, truly I say unto you, unless a grain of wheat falls into the earth
and dies, it remains alone: but if it dies, it bears much fruit.*

John 12:24

 prevalent theme in myths is that life can only take birth from the sacrifice of another life. Violent death is creative in the sense that, in the words of Mircea Eliade, "the life which is sacrificed manifests itself in a more brilliant form upon another plane of existence."[10]

Death is seen not as a definitive end in itself, not an absolute annihilation, as we sometimes think of it. Death is likened to the seed that is sown in the bosom of the earth mother to give birth to new life.

In initiation ceremonies in many cultures, initiates undergo symbolic deaths in order to be reborn with greater wisdom. In these cultures, the people look upon death as the supreme means of spiritual regeneration. This view is also held by the great world religions, including Christianity, in which the participant undergoes a symbolic rebirth. The believer is continually dying in order to be reborn, to grow more through the process of death and rebirth, to become more alive and whole. Death is seen as the continuous ongoing event that leads us closer to the soul, as we change our perspective from the personal to the universal.

According to the Bhagavad Gita (2:12), "Only the bodies, of which this eternal, imperishable, incomprehensible self is the indweller, are said to have an end." It is the human spirit that is capable of infinite growth. And the spirit, or the soul, is nurtured and thrives in the realm of images and symbols. Thus, as Joseph Campbell says, "It has always been the prime function of mythology and rite to supply the symbols that carry the human spirit forward, in counteraction to those other constant human fantasies that tend to tie it back. In fact, it may well be that the very high incidence of neuroticism among ourselves follows from the decline among us of such effective spiritual aid."[11]

Without psychological and

Death is likened to the seed that is sown in the earth to give birth to new life.

177

spiritual traditions to help us meet the crucial stages in our lives, we often find ourselves trapped in the world of our childhood, unable to leave it behind to make the important transitions to adulthood. Especially today, in our youth-oriented culture, it has become more and more difficult to grow up. In our society, the goal is not to grow older and wiser, but rather to remain forever young; not to mature but to stay childlike, protected by our parents, or parent-figures, fulfilling their goals and expectations for our lives instead of identifying and facing our own hopes and dreams.

We are missing rites of passage, which in many cultures are supplied by myth and ritual, to enable us to make the transitions from one stage of life to the next. Without these psychological tools we remain fixed in a perpetual state of out-grown childhood, unable to meet life as we find it and unable to accept our ever-changing selves. The function of rites of passage is to enable the psyche to die to the past in order to be reborn to the future. This is the purpose of the exercises and images included in this book, and this is the meaning of the symbol of Death. After its time of winter, the psyche can be reborn anew, like Persephone, emerging from the underworld.

We begin to die as soon as we are born and the end is linked to the beginning.
Manilius

The Poetic Image

 hrough the poetic image, we can come close to finding all the answers we seek. In poetry, words become windows to a wide scope of impressions and responses, and thought is associated with feeling. Poetic words are loaded with significance and power instead of the familiar emptiness of slogans, clichés, and catchphrases. When a word is used in a predictable, trite way, it loses its meaning and its power to move us. But when the word becomes an image, it becomes filled with significance for us. Suddenly the word/image is alive and filled with content and vitality. It transcends the intellectual and becomes filled with a new reality on a physical level. Only then is it possible to express reality. For instance, if we read the cliché, "motherhood and apply pie," the words do nothing for us. But if we see our own mother baking a pie for us, the image becomes personal and emotionally powerful. The mother image in the cliché takes on all the power of a classic universal image to which we respond with far more intensity than we would to any literal or external kind of experience.

This is the way in which words can be used as powerful tools. Words alone can make us well. The words of poetry, song, and story can call up images that overwhelm our senses with intimate memories and feelings that touch us so deeply that they can affect our lives. These are the words that can give us new insights and the personal understandings that can change us. This is the use of images and metaphors that have the power to heal us and give us peace of mind. This is the power of universal images, which are loaded with symbolism. When we visualize these images and symbols we can find the path that will lead us past our limitations, to growth.

The difference between the literal words of the journalist, lawyer, or ad writer and the symbolism of the poet reflects the difference between the left and the right hemispheres of the brain. The journalist and the lawyer must be rational and logical, organized and factual in order to make a point. The poet, however, reaches into the inner self to pull out memories, feelings, myths, and symbols, to touch us deep at the source of our own feelings and memories. This is why the poet offers us a more immediate reality than all the facts and data commanded by the journalist. The poet's words connect us with our own source of memories and feelings. While time marches by, changing all the facts for the journalist, the poet's words and images are timeless, as true tomorrow as they are today, and far more deeply personal and moving.

Within ourselves, as within the poet's words, all the wisdom, truth, beauty, joy, and power of life are contained. All we need to do is reach down under the surface and pull them out. They exist in a timeless form, always true and always compelling.

We have all had the experience of being struck by a thought or feeling that touches us deeply. It may have been the sight of a child learning to take a first step, or a beautiful flower bud. The moment becomes filled with emotion; tears may come to our eyes. It is at this moment, as we are filled with feeling, that we are in touch with our unlimited capacity to respond to the poignant and the beautiful in the realms that exist beyond words.

When we can use the poetic image to free ourselves from the mechanics that bind us to the literal world and trap our dreams, we can experience a sense of rebirth. A joyous feeling of self-discovery is part of the process of releasing our capacity for creating and experiencing joy. This is the metamorphosis of the butterfly when it comes alive and begins to fly. It is the rebirth of the psyche that has been condemned to the underworld. When we let our dreams fly free, life becomes touching and important, because we have become alive.

Looking at . . .

The Pursuit of Life

This exercise will demonstrate that an emphasis on your end goals is only one part of the larger issue of how to find peace of mind and a sense of fulfillment in your life.

1. Think of a major, long-term, lifetime goal. Write it down on the chart below.

2. Think of ten tasks that will take you to that goal. List them under your goal.

3. For each task you listed, try to find a way in which the task can have some value to you on its own.

The activity that goes into meeting a task may provide you with fulfillment, amusement, enrichment, and enjoyment on its own, without regard to the final goal. These activities will provide something valuable in your life; these are the important items on the list below. Your goal can be reached just once; it is only the direction in which you are traveling, not the trip itself. The trip is made up of the experiences you have along the way.

Major Goal: _____

	Task to Reach the Goal	Value of the Task
1		
2		
3		
4		
5		
6		
7		
8		
9		
10		

Chapter 15
Temperance

he symbol of Temperance represents adapting to the flow of existence and combining all the elements of your life in order to keep a harmonious balance. It stands for the tempering of all things in order to create harmony.

Looking at . . .

The Angel of Temperance

he guardian angel stands with one foot in the water and one foot upon the land. A time of new beginnings is at hand. This is the time of confidence and optimism. Miracles will now come to pass. We will receive great gifts and faith as we continue the process of inner evolution.

The angel pours the waters of inspiration from the silver chalice of the moon into the gold chalice of the sun, in order to: _____

_____

The angel says to you:

I give you _____

You will _____

You can _____

If you should become lost on your journey, just _____

The name of the angel is _____

The angel represents the guidance we can receive from the unconscious. The moon and the sun, silver and gold, are symbols of the two principles, left and right, yin and yang, male and female. When they are poured together they become purified.

This exercise will give you some insight about who this angel is for you and some messages from your unconscious.

The angel in the picture of Temperance is blending the powers of the sun and the moon. She understands the benefit of science tempered by ethics, and of knowledge combined with character. Her message is that we can take charge of our own destinies when we claim sole responsibility for our acts.

Say to yourself:
I integrate and blend the diverse elements of my life to create a balance, unity, and harmony in everything I do. My life is filled with joy and good health.

Looking at . . .

The Eye of the Triangle

The wisdom of the eye in the triangle speaks to you. It says:

You are _____

You can _____

You must _____

You will _____

You have _____

The eye in the triangle in this exercise represents omniscience. The wisdom of the eye gives you insights from your own inner, all-knowing wisdom.

Listen to this wisdom from within. It is your guiding spirit, the source of your own highest guidance and greatest understanding.

Looking at . . .

The Flag

Write down the motto that belongs in the flag above: _____

What are the colors of the flag? _____

What picture belongs on the flag? _____

You may want to draw the picture and color the flag above.

> The flag represents self-assertion and identity. In the color index at the back of the book, look up the significance of the colors you chose for your flag. What can you find out about yourself from your choices.

Looking at . . .

The Cup

You have found a cup along the road where you are walking.

What does the cup look like? _____

Where did it come from? _____

How do you feel about it? _____

What will you do with it? _____

The cup, or chalice, represents the fullness of life, the riches and joys of living. Your response to this exercise will indicate how you feel about abundance contained in the draught of life.

Gandhi's Seven Sins

The idea of a balance of qualities that create a harmonious whole is reflected by Mahatma Gandhi, who wrote that there were seven sins in the world:

1. Wealth without work

2. Pleasure without conscience

3. Knowledge without character

4. Commerce without morality

5. Science without humanity

6. Worship without sacrifice

7. Politics without principle

In the following story, the heroine is able to integrate the masculine and the feminine, the courageous and the clever, the explicit and the implied aspects of her nature.

The Story of Mizilca

ong ago there lived an old knight who was a skilled magician. He led a quiet, peaceful life with his wife and three daughters, until the sultan sent a message commanding him to come and serve him for a year and a day. If he could not come, he was to send his son.

The old man grieved day and night, for he was aged and lame and had no son to send in his place. When his daughters saw how sad he was they asked him, "Have we done something to displease you?"

"Oh no," the old man replied. "I am worried because the sultan has commanded me to come and serve him for a year and a day. If I cannot do this I am dishonored, but I am old and lame and I have no son to send in my place."

"I am young and healthy. I will dress up as a boy and go in your place," replied the eldest daughter. So she had her long hair cut off and she dressed in a man's clothes and set off with her father's horse and armor. But her father secretly rode out ahead until he came to a bridge. There he changed himself into a blue boar and hid, waiting for his daughter. When she arrived the boar charged at her. She screamed in terror and turned around and galloped back to the castle.

Next, the knight's second daughter begged to be sent to serve in her father's place. So the old man gave her his horse and armor, and she set off for the sultan's palace. Again the old knight went ahead and hid among the trees waiting for his daughter. When she arrived, a lion leapt out at her. She screamed and galloped back home.

Then the knight's youngest daughter asked to be sent to serve in her father's place. "My dear Mizilca, how can you hope to succeed when your sisters have all failed? Stay home and keep your long hair," he told her. But Mizilca insisted that she be sent, so her father gave her an old horse and a rusty sword and sent her off. Once again her father rode off ahead and hid among the trees.

When Mizilca came to the bridge, a dragon leapt out at her, breathing smoke and fire. Mizilca was brave and did not falter. She galloped right at the dragon, which ran away into the woods. Mizilca crossed the bridge and rode on.

When she arrived at the palace, Mizilca told the sultan that she was the old knight's son, come to serve him for a year and a day. The sultan suspected she was no lad at all but a maiden, but he welcomed her into his company of knights.

As the weeks passed, the sultan saw that Mizilca could ride and fight and shoot the bow and arrow, but still when he looked at her he thought she was no man. The sultan went to a wise old woman and asked her how he could find out if Mizilca was a lad or a maiden. The woman told him to arrange a bazaar with silks and jewels on one side and weapons and armor on the other. If she were a maiden, she would look at the finery and ignore the weapons, the old woman told him.

But Mizilca was not to be fooled. She ignored the silks and jewels and admired the weapons.

As time went on, Mizilca proved herself to be brave, loyal, and strong. Still, the sultan could not believe that she was a man. He went again to the wise woman, who told him to hide some pearls in Mizilca's oatmeal. "If she is a maiden, she will save them, if she is not she will spit them out," the old woman said.

Suspecting the trick, Mizilca spat out the pearls as if they were stones.

At last a year and a day passed and it was time for Mizilca to return home. As the sultan bid her farewell, he said, "You have served me well, but tell me, are you a youth or a maiden?" Mizilca did not answer. She mounted her horse and as she rode off she called out:

> High and mighty sultan, praised be!
> Though your word is law o'er land and sea
> I know more of you than you of me!

This story illustrates the great potential for strength and courage the inner mind, represented by the younger daughter, possesses. This courage can assist us in facing the challenges of life. The inner self does indeed know more of us than we of it. When we elicit the aid of our inner power in our adventures, we find that we, too, possess new powers and strengths.

The angel of Temperance reminds us that we each possess all the resources we need to meet any challenge, and we can discover hidden capabilities when we learn to balance our perspective and to integrate the divergent elements of life into a harmonious whole.

The angel is guidance from the unconscious, or a message from God.

Reflections . . .

More Information, Less Wisdom

n this day of complex technology, we are faced with an overabundance of information, but we have not developed the sophistication to discriminate the true from the false, the relative from the specific, the relevant from the irrelevant. We watch the news at least once a day, we watch videos, listen to the radio, read magazines and books, hear tapes, c.d.s, and records, talk on the telephone, and many of us have our own computers. We have limitless information available, but often we do not really know what to do with it.

We are told that information will be the basis of much of the industry of the future. We will all have videodiscs and videotexts, home computers, and "intelligent" telephones. The experts say we are moving from a society of mass consumption of centrally produced goods to an information-based economy. Whereas a hundred years ago 40 percent of the workers in the U.S. were agricultural, today more people are involved in the production and distribution of information than are working in agriculture, mining, manu-  facturing, and service combined. The largest contributor to the gross national product is not goods or services but information.

The computer experts say that one major problem of an information society is the difficulty of making sense of the unlimited amounts of information available to us. As one journalist put it, "Where can we find wisdom in an age where information is cheaper than thought?"

Everything that was ever written about a particular subject can be displayed on the screen of a computer. But how can we discriminate the meaningful from the meaningless? We are being bombarded with data, making the job of finding answers and reaching conclusions far more difficult than it has ever been before.

The problem is that of discrimination, sorting out the important information from volumes of extraneous facts. This process is not an analytical one; rather it is the function of the other mode of thinking, the right side of the brain, the process that sees the whole picture and makes sense of it in the face of mountains of fragmented data.

If making sense out of bare fact is the job of the right brain, we may be turning a corner in the intellectual development of our culture. Perhaps the new information systems will force us to rediscover the usefulness of the right-brain processes of synthesizing and generalizing, which could enable us to view life in less fragmented, biased, and mechanistic ways on all levels. We could learn to integrate

---

Reflections . . .

More Information, Less Wisdom

n this day of complex technology, we are faced with an overabundance of information, but we have not developed the sophistication to discriminate the true from the false, the relative from the specific, the relevant from the irrelevant. We watch the news at least once a day, we watch videos, listen to the radio, read magazines and books, hear tapes, c.d.s, and records, talk on the telephone, and many of us have our own computers. We have limitless information available, but often we do not really know what to do with it.

We are told that information will be the basis of much of the industry of the future. We will all have videodiscs and videotexts, home computers, and "intelligent" telephones. The experts say we are moving from a society of mass consumption of centrally produced goods to an information-based economy. Whereas a hundred years ago 40 percent of the workers in the U.S. were agricultural, today more people are involved in the production and distribution of information than are working in agriculture, mining, manu-  facturing, and service combined. The largest contributor to the gross national product is not goods or services but information.

The computer experts say that one major problem of an information society is the difficulty of making sense of the unlimited amounts of information available to us. As one journalist put it, "Where can we find wisdom in an age where information is cheaper than thought?"

Everything that was ever written about a particular subject can be displayed on the screen of a computer. But how can we discriminate the meaningful from the meaningless? We are being bombarded with data, making the job of finding answers and reaching conclusions far more difficult than it has ever been before.

The problem is that of discrimination, sorting out the important information from volumes of extraneous facts. This process is not an analytical one; rather it is the function of the other mode of thinking, the right side of the brain, the process that sees the whole picture and makes sense of it in the face of mountains of fragmented data.

If making sense out of bare fact is the job of the right brain, we may be turning a corner in the intellectual development of our culture. Perhaps the new information systems will force us to rediscover the usefulness of the right-brain processes of synthesizing and generalizing, which could enable us to view life in less fragmented, biased, and mechanistic ways on all levels. We could learn to integrate

190

ethics and social responsibility into our businesses and value the quality of our lives as much as we value our net worth, by learning to utilize the processes of the right brain in problem solving and decision making.

As our society becomes more and more complex, along with having more information available we will also be faced with the necessity of making more choices. With increased choices we will have added responsibility. The more we become capable of knowing, the more we will have to decide how to use what we know. Thus, the era of information is also the era of increased personal responsibility as each of us is faced with more and more data to sort through and accept or reject, act upon or forget. The more we know, the more we must decide what we will do about our knowledge.

Personal Responsibility

y assuming responsibility for what we do, we are also taking on the responsibility for what happens to us. Thus the idea of responsibility is a frame of mind or an attitude that begins with the way we think and extends beyond ourselves to our relationship with others and affects all the experiences and circumstances of our lives.

The idea of taking responsibility begins with an acceptance of ourselves as being worthy of happiness and fulfillment. Then we must love our neighbors as ourselves, participating in the common experience of life and sharing the responsibility of human existence. By loving our neighbors we express our understanding that we all share the same earth and the same mortality; that we are all one another's neighbors. When we accept ourselves as we are, we can accept others as they are.

Individual strength comes from our ability to take hold of life, accepting ourselves and accepting existence in an active, positive way. Being passive and fatalistic may sometimes seem to be the easy way out of assuming responsibility, but when we excuse everything as misfortune and accident, we assume the role of the powerless victim. It is only when we assume responsibility for our lives that we have the power to find solutions. Our claim to personal responsibility is our only claim to personal power.

We are each capable of great strength, but in order to tap that strength we need to accept our own primary role as the leader of our own life's experiences. We also need to accept life on its own terms, accepting hardship, pain, and suffering as natural parts of life. When we expect to undergo life's challenges in order to grow, we will find that we have become the hero in our own life's drama and we will be rewarded with strength, happiness, and fulfillment.

Step V in Review

In Step V you entered into the realms of death, where you met with the Hanged Man, Death, and Temperance. Write down a brief summary of what these three images have taught you about the nature and meaning of death and of self-sacrifice, change, and adaptation.

Write down the most important feelings and insights you have gained from your pilgrimage into the realms of death.

Step VI
Confrontation with the Devil

The time has come when you must confront the devil,
or the hidden, shadow side of your psyche. This is the
only way for you to go past your deepest fears and
angers and other barriers that hinder your progress.

After you have come to terms with the devil and all the
demons that haunt you, you can be born anew, with
a higher understanding of yourself, your life, and the
world. Thus you progress on the path to
self-realization.

Chapter 16
The Devil

 basic mythic theme is that of the descent into the underworld, where the hero explores the realms of death and comes to terms with the Devil, which is the shadow or negative side of the personality. It has been said that the shadow continually follows the body of one who walks in the sun. This is the time to confront the shadow and come to terms with it.

The hero returns to the underworld or to the inner earth, mother nature, the earth mother. This is the stage at which the seed germinates; the hero must spend a certain amount of time in the underworld before he or she can be born again to reemerge into the waking world, bringing back new insight or new knowledge.

Looking at . . .

The Devil

ou are enveloped in a great darkness as black as the bottom of the sea, as black as the center of the earth. You are in the land of night and the land of shadows where there are great dangers, for this is the realm of the Devil.

A dim red flame burns in the distance, and you can see the outline of a figure. You are drawn toward the figure, and as you approach it you realize this is the Devil himself. He says, "I am the prince of falsehood, I am the prince of lies."

The Devil catches you and places a chain around your neck. Then he tells you:

_____

He says, I hold you in bondage all the days of your life, but the chains that hold

you are made of your own _____

What does the devil look like? _____

What color are his clothes? _____

You can be freed, but first you must _____

The Devil says: I am the Devil, my name is _____

I am from _____

I have _____

I will _____

My power comes from _____

You can tame me by _____

The Devil represents the fear and ignorance of superficial thinking. This exercise will identify for you the source of these feelings and how to become freed of them.

The devil is fear and ignorance, as we encounter him along our path.

The Devil begat darkness, darkness begat ignorance.
Martin Luther, Table Talk, 67

Say to yourself:
I will transcend the darkness of ignorance
and overcome the chaos of my deepest fears.

Looking at . . . *Going into the Midnight River*

In the black of night you reach a river's edge. You are pulled into the icy waters. As you gasp for air, you see a creature emerging from the depths.

It says to you:

My name is _____

I am _____

I will _____

I exist because of _____

I will take you to _____

There you must learn the great lesson, which is _____

Your task is to _____

Your reward will be _____

_____

The water is your unconscious. The creature is the Devil, or your shadow side. This exercise will help you understand some of the secrets hidden from your literal, conscious mind. These are the secrets that cause you to do things and react in ways that surprise you and seem, on the surface, to be entirely opposite to the way you think you should react or expect yourself to respond.

The water is your unconscious. The creature on the right is the Devil, or the shadow side. The bird represents the soul.

Feeling Lost and Forsaken

Dante described the feeling of being lost and forsaken, having strayed from the path of truth, in *The Inferno*, Canto 1.

> In the midway of this mortal life
> I found that I was in a dusky wood;
> For from the straight path I had gone astray.
> Ah me! How hard a thing it is to tell
> The wildness of that rough and savage place.
> The very thought of which brings back my fear!
> So bitter was it, death is little more:
> But that the good I found there may be told
> I will describe the other things I saw.
> How I entered there I can scarcely say,
> So weary was my mind, so filled with sleep
> I reeled and wandered from the path of truth . . .[12]

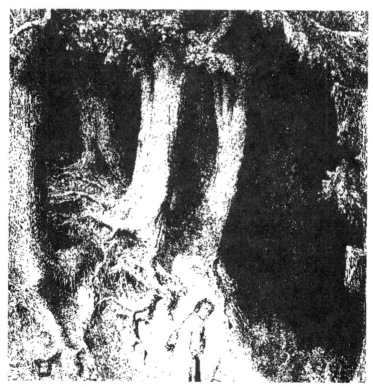

. . . lost and forsaken in a dusky wood, having wandered from the path of truth.

In the following fable, three soldiers find themselves face-to-face with the Devil, who intends to take them away with him.

The Devil and His Grandmother

A war was being fought. The king had many soldiers but he paid them too little to live on. Three of the soldiers got together and decided to desert. "If we're caught they'll string us up on the gallows. How can we escape?" one of them asked.

The second soldier said, "Let's hide in that wheat field, where nobody will see us. The troops aren't allowed in it and tomorrow they'll be moving on." So the three deserters crept into the wheat field. But the troops didn't move on, they stayed camped on all sides. The deserters spent two days and nights in the field, until they were so hungry they almost died. But to come out would mean certain death.

Suddenly, a fiery dragon came flying through the air and stopped in the field where the soldiers hid. It asked them why they were hiding. "We're three soldiers who have deserted because the pay was too low to live on, and now we will starve to death if we stay here, or die on the gallows if we come out," they explained.

"If you promise to serve me for seven years," said the dragon, "I'll carry you over the army and no one will catch you." The soldiers agreed to this, since they had no other choice.

Now, the dragon was really none other than the Devil himself. When he delivered the soldiers to a far-off country, the Devil gave each soldier a little whip and said, "Just swish it and snap it and all the money you could wish for will come popping out of the ground. All you will have to do is pick it up. You'll be able to live like lords, keep horses and ride in carriages. But at the end of seven years you will belong to me." Then he gave them a book to sign. "Before I take you away," he told them, "I'll give you one last chance. I'll ask you a riddle. If you guess the answer, you'll be free and I will have no further power over you." With that the dragon flew away and the three soldiers started off with their little whips.

With plenty of money now, the soldiers lived in comfort and luxury. Time passed quickly. But as the seven years drew to a close, two of the soldiers were overcome with a black fear. The third soldier told them, "Don't worry, brothers, all problems can be solved if we have faith and work hard. We will find an answer to the riddle."

The third soldier set out in search of the answer to the riddle. In the fields he met an old woman who asked him what he was searching for. The soldier told her how they had served the Devil for seven years and now he would take them away if they didn't have an answer to this riddle.

The old woman told him to search in the forest for a hut shaped like a rock. This was the Devil's home. The soldier finally found the hut and met an old woman inside. He told her his story and she took pity on him. She told him to hide in the cellar and listen. Then the old grandmother went about fixing the Devil his dinner. When the Devil came flying home at midnight she asked, "Did you catch many souls today?"

The Devil said, "Not today, but I will have the souls of the three soldiers soon. After I ask them my riddle, I will take them away."

"What is the riddle?" asked the grandmother.

"Just this," said the Devil. "A dead rabbit-fish from the North Sea will be their roast, a whale's rib will be their silver spoon, and a hollow horse's hoof will be their wine glass."

In the morning the soldier slipped out of the cellar, thanked the grandmother, and returned to his friends. He told them the answers to the Devil's riddle.

When the Devil came to get them he said, "Now you will come with me unless you can guess what kind of meal I will serve you."

The first soldier said, "You will serve a dead rabbit-fish from the North Sea."

The second soldier said, "You will use a whale's rib for a silver spoon."

And the third soldier said, "A hollow horse's hoof will be your wine glass." At that the Devil flew away in a rage, for he had lost his power over the three.

In this story the self (or the third soldier) was able to come to terms with the dark forces (or the Devil) by understanding its secrets.

Often we feel lost and forsaken because of our mistaken idea of our place in the universe. It is a false and groundless fear; we do not have to be slaves to necessity and chance. The forces in life that seem to bring adversity can actually bring us great benefits when we learn to overcome them.

The dragon, or the Devil, is our ego and greed, which may be overcome through self-understanding.

The Story of Jonah and the Whale

he prophet Jonah was commanded by God to preach to the people in a distant land, in the city of Nineveh. Jonah did not want to go to Nineveh. He went to the coast and boarded a ship headed for Tarshish, which was in the opposite direction.

After they had been several days at sea, a great storm threatened to wreck the ship. Jonah realized that the storm was his punishment from God for disobeying His command. He told the ship's crew what he had done, and he said to them, "Throw me into the sea and the storm will stop." But the men pitied Jonah. They decided to try to row the ship back to land instead. However, the harder they rowed, the more the sea raged.

Finally the men decided that the only way to save the ship was to throw Jonah overboard. As soon as they did so, the storm ceased and the sea became calm.

Jonah was tossed about in the sea until a large whale appeared and swallowed him. For three days and nights Jonah remained alive inside the belly of the whale, praying to God for forgiveness. Then the whale opened his mouth and delivered Jonah onto dry land. After that, Jonah went to Nineveh, to do God's work.

Jonah was swallowed and taken down into the belly of the whale.

The Night Sea Journey

The story of Jonah and the whale follows a classic mythic theme of the night sea journey in which the hero goes into a whale's belly and finally comes out again, transformed. The whale is a womb image symbolizing the greatness and power of life that has been hidden in the unconscious and has overwhelmed the conscious personality. The hero is swallowed up into the unknown, where he seems to have died. The passage across this threshold is a form of self-annihilation in which the hero goes inward, later to be born anew.

This story is a metaphor for the hero's psychological state of depression, which forces him to pay attention to his unconscious. He leaves the realms of the known and familiar, where he feels oriented, to go off to the edges of the unknown, which is the lake or the sea. Here a monster from beneath the sea comes to meet him.

In the story, Jonah was swallowed and taken down into the whale's belly. This represents the conscious personality coming in touch with the unconscious, where all the rules are different and the conscious is no longer in control of things. Thus the hero is forced to undergo the trials and perils of a night sea journey in order to come to terms with himself.

In some night sea stories, the hero comes into conflict with the power of the dark and kills it, as St. George did the dragon. But if the unconscious, or the dragon, is vanquished, the conscious mind takes total control and the person loses touch with his human, creative, physical, and natural parts, and he is no longer a whole person. On the other hand, if the dragon of the unconscious mind wins the battle, the hero becomes devoured by his irrational and ego-driven compulsions. So the challenge is to find a balance between the two realms; that balance is the center of the self.

It has been said that in order to rule nature it is necessary to first learn to obey her laws. Until then, we will be held in bondage by ignorance. To deny our dark side would be foolish as well as destructive. Instead, we must acknowledge and grapple with the beast, for the beast is within. We cannot kill it but we can understand it. Once we understand it we can direct it, through our admission of personal responsibility for it.

Self-Discipline

nherent in the concept of personal responsibility and self-direction is self-discipline, the ability to train ourselves in habits that will contribute to our happiness, success, and well-being.

It takes determination to overcome inertia. Once activity begins, it progresses almost by itself, but getting started requires self-discipline. Without self-discipline, we cannot accomplish anything. However, when we discipline ourselves in one area of life, it becomes easier to discipline ourselves in other areas because we feel stronger and better about ourselves. The strength and pride of our accomplishments encourages us to take on more and greater goals. We feel good about ourselves when we know we can overcome our demons. When we realize that we ourselves possess the power to control our own lives, we find that we can use that power to accomplish anything.

It is easy to fool ourselves and to do a poor job. But soon we become frustrated that we did not meet our goals, and we may give up. This is part of a pattern of withholding our best efforts, of saving our energy and not completely giving ourselves to the challenges at hand. Perhaps we tell ourselves that the goal isn't really worth our best efforts. We are, of course, shortchanging ourselves when we give only what is convenient. Why should we expect the greatest results for less than our greatest efforts? If we do less than our best, it is our own life that will be less than it could have been.

When we fight against our demons, they can become the source of our greatest advantages. However, although we must learn to come to terms with them, they must not be annihilated.

The Uses of Humor

Strife is the creator of all things.

Heraclitus

The Devil can be seen as the wrathful, destructive force in life. And yet, this force is important.

When you are hanging on to your ego in self-centeredness, you are vulnerable to all the frustrations, agonies, and hopelessness of the material world. You can never achieve enough or accumulate enough. You may spend your time regretting the past, but you can never have a better yesterday.

In ancient rituals and dramatic ceremonies, the Devil was often represented as a fool, a jester, or a comic character. This trickster is an aspect of the Devil, doing dirty tricks just when everything is going along fine. The trickster is the serpent in the Garden of Eden, tempting Eve with the apple just when everything seemed to be perfect.

The trickster is also the clown who makes us laugh at ourselves, our troubles, and our foolishness. When we laugh, we let go of the grip of the ego and for a moment we can accept life on its own terms. Humor is the counterbalance to the ego, and laughter improves everything.

The trickster is also the clown who makes us laugh at ourselves and our troubles.

When life gets too difficult to deal with, we instinctively find something to laugh at. In fact, nature's own remedy for inner conflict and the complexities of life is laughter. Laughing at ourselves can be relaxing and even healing. When we laugh and the ego relaxes its hold, we can more easily accept our own frailties and the weaknesses of others. Humor enables us to see things in a new light and to find new answers to our problems.

Laughter is usually provoked by our weaknesses and pettinesses. We laugh at our foibles, and when we laugh, our mental conflicts dissolve. Laughing is the natural emotional and physical antidote to tension, and it is one of the finest capabilities we possess for survival in a complicated world.

We take ourselves and our interests so seriously that we often forget the rest of the world's needs. In addition, tangible material reality is the only one we have accepted while the rest of life has been lost, undermined, and overlooked. This has led us to a world in which personal competitiveness, consumption, and status have become our predominant values.

By laughing at negative forces, or the Devil wherever he appears, whether it is in ourselves, in others, or in the world, we are utilizing an instinctive tool for survival. A sense of the comic in life is one of the great treasures from within that can save us.

The Devil, or the trickster, reminds us that if we would change our lives, we must do so ourselves, and one way to begin is to laugh at ourselves and our vanities, which deprives them of their power over us.

When we laugh at our vanities we deprive them of their power over us.

The next two exercises show you ways to use humor to deal with something that has been bothering you.

Looking at . . .

The Paradoxical Intention

In this exercise, you wish for the very thing you most fear. This breaks your anticipatory anxiety, which is usually the source of tension.

We worry and anticipate all sorts of dreadful things. Whether they actually happen or not, we have poisoned our bodies with worry. To break this habit of worrying, simply wish for the extreme of whatever it is that you fear. Fantasize the situation to the point of absurdity; joke about it; talk about the extreme results you are fantasizing. Listen to how silly you sound and laugh at yourself. Make your exaggeration humorous and let other people laugh at it. Then, instead of waiting and expecting the worst, you will be confronting your fears and laughing at them.

1. On a separate piece of paper or in your journal, write down whatever it is that you most fear or dread.

2. Close your eyes and imagine that what you wrote down has really happened. Imagine the details vividly.

3. Exaggerate the situation in your mind—imagine it to the extreme point of absurdity.

4. Find the ridiculous in what you have imagined. Let yourself see the humor in its foolishness.

5. Let yourself laugh at your mental picture of this *reductio ad absurdum*. You may even go so far as to publicly relate your story and let others laugh at it with you. In this way you will be able to confront the demon and transform it into a joke.

Exaggerate the situation that bothers you, to the point of absurdity.

Desensitization Using Humor

For this exercise you will need five index cards. On each card, write down one aspect of a problem that is bothering you. On the first card write down step one, the mildest aspect of the problem, that portion of the problem that is the easiest for you to deal with. On a second card write down step two, the next hardest aspect of the problem. Continue until you have broken the problem or worry into five steps ranging from its mildest to its most severe aspect.

For example, if you were worried about money you might write "buying a new car" on card one. Since this is not a life-threatening issue, you could put it off a while or buy a used car. You might write "buying groceries" on card two, since this is a very real need, but you can probably get by by economizing and not starve. You could write "paying the mortgage" (or "the rent") for card three, since this is a major expense that cannot be put off. When you get to card five you might write "finding a better job," since this may well be the basis of your problem and would probably be your greatest source of anxiety.

1. Start with the first card. Think of all the silliest things you can imagine. In the example above, the first card deals with buying a car. You could imagine that you buy some kind of oddball car. When you can see an image that makes you laugh, write it down on card one. The next card has to do with buying groceries. You could say that you plan to write a cookbook on cooking with cat food; it would include recipes for cat-food pancakes, cat-food cake, and so on. Think of some silly extreme that makes you laugh. Write it on card two.

You can overcome fears and phobias by imagining them associated with something comical.

2. Continue with each card, imagining any zany solution to the problem. The images should be so ridiculous that you are amused instead of anxious. As you progress with the cards, the images should get funnier and funnier with the progressing seriousness of the situation. For instance, with finding a new job, you should dream up the most ridiculous and funny images you can possibly imagine, then write them on card five.

3. Now sit quietly in a relaxed position. Close your eyes and relax as deeply as possible, letting your mind just drift. Once you are deeply relaxed, begin with card one. Read the card and visualize the humorous image you wrote on it.

4. After you have been able to laugh at or at least to feel amused by the first card, go on to the next card. Continue until you have gone through all five cards. If you start to feel anxious, go back to the previous card. Do not go on to the next card until you feel you are ready to do so in a completely relaxed state of mind. When you feel any discomfort, redirect the response into laughter.

This exercise is especially useful for overcoming fears or phobias. The gradual, imagined exposure associated with something comical will enable you to become accustomed to the object of your fears step-by-step in a safe, nonthreatening way.

Find ways to redirect your anxiety into laughter.

The next two exercises are designed to bring up memories and ideas from the inner mind, to help you develop an increased sense of responsibility and control over life.

Looking at . . .

Exercise for Dealing with Life

Fill in the boxes below.

List five life events that you remember with regret or sorrow.	Write something that each event has taught you.	What are you still learning from this experience?	In what ways can this experience improve your life in the future?
1			
2			
3			
4			
5			

Looking at . . .

Exercise for Dealing with the Present

List three things that make you unhappy.	Write something that each of these things can teach you.	How can this situation or experience improve your life?
1		
2		
3		
Write down one way you can assume more responsibility for each situation listed above.	What is the ideal result of your increased responsibility?	How can you take on more responsibility in order to reach your goal?
1		
2		
3		

Chapter 17
The Tower

he two people who are forcibly ejected from the Tower in the picture were prisoners of their intellect and their strivings for power, the literal and material side of their natures. They had lost contact with their ground of being and the fluid waters of their inmost nature. Then they were confronted with the inadequacy of their human perceptions in the face of nature's elemental powers. The lightning gave them the opportunity for a sudden glimpse of truth, a flash of inspiration, a breakthrough.

Inside the Tower

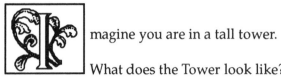 magine you are in a tall tower.

What does the Tower look like? _____

How do you feel inside the Tower? _____

What do you do inside? _____

Why are you in the Tower? _____

List three ways you could get out:

1 _____

2 _____

3 _____

The Tower represents your imprisonment and sense of isolation. What you find inside symbolizes what you keep hidden within. This exercise will give you some ideas about the nature of your inner secrets and how to free yourself from your sense of isolation.

Looking at . . .

The Fall from the Tower

 man and woman are trapped in the Tower, where it is cold, damp, and dark. Suddenly the sky lights up as a bolt of lightning strikes the top of the Tower. Fire blazes toward the heavens and the two people are hurled from the Tower to the ground.

Finish the following sentences:

I was imprisoned in the Tower because of my _____

The lightning that struck the Tower came from _____

After my fall from the Tower, I will be _____

The Tower is made of my own _____

Now that I am free, I will _____

I have learned that _____

The Tower represents the hidden forces in your inner mind, and also the mistaken belief that you are isolated from life and from others. Lightning strikes the tower to destroy ignorance and free the prisoners trapped within.

The two people in the Tower are the male and female aspects of your psyche. They have become disconnected from their inner depths and are thrown over. Psychologically they experience this overthrowing as a state of depression, which forces them into a reevaluation of their lifestyles and values.

Your responses to this exercise should give you an idea of the source of your own experience of depression and need for a new perspective.

Say to yourself:
With a flash of insight I am freed of the limitations of my old mental habits.
I discover new wisdom in a breakthrough of understanding.

Looking at . . .

The Two Towers

 magine you see two towers ahead of you.

What is inside the towers? _____

How do you feel about these towers? _____

What do they seem to represent to you? _____

What lies beyond the towers? _____

These two towers are hiding places for your secrets. This exercise indicates how you feel about these secrets and their significance to you. What you see beyond the towers is a symbol of your growth and liberation.

Maid Maleen

nce upon a time there was a great king's daughter whose name was Maid Maleen. This princess loved a young prince, but her father insisted that she marry the neighboring king's son. Maid Maleen refused to marry the prince of her father's choice. In a rage, her father decreed that she was to be shut up inside a tower for seven years.

Food and drink sufficient for seven years were brought to the tower for Maid Maleen and her lady-in-waiting, and the two were led inside. Then the door was walled up behind them.

Maid Maleen's prince rode around and around the tower many times, calling to her, but the walls were so thick that no sound could come through. Finally, believing she was dead, the prince departed.

Time passed slowly for the princess and her lady-in-waiting. They could tell that time was passing by their dwindling food supply. Finally, when they were out of food, the princess expected to hear the sounds of the king's men knocking down the walls to set them free.

But there was no sound. The princess thought her father must have forgotten her, so she decided to try to dig her way out. She and her lady-in-waiting took turns scraping the dirt. Suddenly a bolt of lightning struck the tower and the wall crumbled.

In the snowy night the two young women saw that the castle and all the kingdom for as far as the eye could see lay in ruins. In the morning, they began to wander toward the edges of the kingdom, across bleak and charred countryside. At night they slept under hedges, and they found berries to eat.

Finally they came to a kingdom at the seacoast. There they were able to find work as scullery maids in the castle. As it so happened, this was the very kingdom of the prince whom Maid Maleen had loved seven years before. For those seven years the prince had mourned for her, but finally he had agreed to his parents' wishes that he marry. He had consented to marry whomever they chose, saying it no longer mattered to him. His parents chose a very rich princess who was also very coldhearted. The coldness of her heart showed in her unattractive face.

The wedding was arranged, but the bride had not yet shown herself for fear the prince would change his mind. She stayed in her rooms and took her meals there.

On the wedding day the princess said to Maid Maleen, who brought her meals, "You will wear my gown and take my place today, so the prince will not change his mind before the ceremony. You may not say a word to the prince. Afterward, I will take my rightful place by his side." Maid Maleen protested that the scheme would not be fair, but the princess insisted, saying, "Be quiet or I will have your head cut off!"

So Maid Maleen put on the bridal gown and swore she would say no word to man or woman that day. The prince greeted her courteously, looking at her with surprise and interest, but she said not a word. He thought she must be very shy as he led her to the church.

On the way, Maid Maleen said to a nettle bush, "Nettles stand aside, for I am the true bride."

"What did you say?" asked the prince. But Maid Maleen said not a word.

When they reached the edge of the sea, she said, "Sea hold back your tide, for I am the true bride."

"What did you say?" asked the prince, but Maid Maleen said not a word.

When they reached the church, Maleen said, "Church doors open wide, for I am the true bride." Then the priest joined their hands and they were married. The prince put a gold ring on Maleen's finger, and he kissed her and led her back to the palace for the wedding supper and dancing.

The princess smiled at the prince but said not a word. She returned the bridal gown and put on her kitchen rags, but she kept the ring for it fit her finger too tightly to be removed.

That night when the prince came to the room of the coldhearted princess, she veiled her face and dimmed the lamps. "What did you say to the nettle bush today?" he asked her.

"I do not talk to bushes," the princess replied scornfully.

"What did you say to the sea?" he asked.

"I do not talk to the sea," she told him.

"What did you say to the church doors?" he asked.

"I do not speak to doors," she scoffed.

"Then you are not the true bride," said the prince.

"Oh yes I am," answered the princess in a rage.

"Where is the ring I put upon your finger?" asked the prince.

"I lost it," the princess replied.

The prince pulled aside her veil and was shocked to find she was a different woman than the one he had just married. "Who are you and how did you get here? What has happened to my true bride?" he demanded.

"I was ill so I sent my servant in my place today," the princess replied.

"Send for her, I would like to see her," the prince demanded.

The coldhearted princess agreed, but secretly she told the guards to execute Maleen at once, saying, "She is a thief, she has stolen my wedding ring."

The guards seized Maid Maleen, but she yelled out so loudly the prince heard her. He rushed to the courtyard and ordered the guards to release her. "Who are you?" he asked. "You are the very image of my beloved Maid Maleen, who died in a tower seven years ago."

"I am Maid Maleen," she answered. "I was shut up in the tower, but I did not die. When I escaped seven years later, my father's kingdom was destroyed and I wandered across the countryside until I reached this castle."

The prince rejoiced and embraced his true bride. He ordered the coldhearted princess to be sent home.

Together, the prince and Maid Maleen ruled the land for many, many years. The tower remained standing. As children passed it, they would sing:

> Sunflower, moonflower,
> Who sits inside the tower?
> Within there sits a princess fair.
> Nobody can find her there.
> No storm can make the tower fall,
> But lightning can break down the wall.
> Oak tree, willow tree,
> Come and follow after me.

The inner self is trapped inside the tower.

In this story the princess, or the inner self, is trapped within the tower, which represents the limitations and repressions of the material world. After lightning strikes and she is freed, she can finally overcome the obstacles that had kept her from her true love, or fulfillment. The lightning is a symbol for the flash of insight that can free us from self-limiting ideas.

The Purpose of Depression

n a psychological state of depression we feel heavy and lifeless, without ambition or creative energy. However, this is an important state to experience, because when it happens to us it indicates that deeper layers of our personality have been pushed down until they can no longer be reached. The state of depression indicates that we are out of touch with important parts of ourselves.

Often a creative person will experience profound depression before beginning a new piece of work, or at some time during the work. This happens because the person has overlooked some important creative forces, which have then become buried in the unconscious.

We often feel that our depression is based on anger or frustration because we have failed to reach our material desires. However, a true sense of self-fulfillment can only be spiritual. The state of depression actually signals an opportunity for a new perspective that will enable us to find new directions and priorities.

With depression comes the opportunity to reestablish a link with our buried longings so we can pull up repressed information that will become the basis for a personal breakthrough. This is the significance of the symbol of the Tower.

This woodcut by Albrecht Dürer shows the apocalypse, a powerful medieval theme of the end of the world. This state of physical and mental chaos is known psychologically as depression.

The Age of Information

In this age of sophisticated computer technology, we have deprived ourselves of much of our inner strength and wisdom. The type of information available to us today, even with the most advanced computer technology, is just a shuffling and reshuffling of known data. We are no closer to truly original and important insights than we were before the day of the computer. No equation and no program, no matter how sophisticated, even if it has gathered and analyzed all data, can understand the nature of reality.

In the complexity, confusion, and cynicism of our era, our sense of the dramatic quality of reality as it is unfolding at this moment has been pushed aside. What we think of as reality is what is reported on the front pages of the newspapers, even though that material is no longer true; things have changed since it was written. As we observed in an earlier chapter, time alters everything. What we read about tonight has become history; it is no longer an accurate report of what is going on at this moment. As a result, although we may feel we have abundant information, in fact we have only one person's or one newspaper's or one TV network's rendition of fact, and even that has become obsolete by the time it gets to us.

Furthermore, the language in which our newspapers are written is a linear, external mode of expression that cannot describe the real inner complexities of experience for which there are no words. Thus we are left with impressions about reality that are inaccurate, distorted, limited, and often cynical.

We are constantly being bombarded by an increasing overload of facts. We educate our children in the facts—they must learn lists of names, dates, places, and numbers. But with all this information, we do not come any closer to understanding the truly important elements of existence, such as why we are here, what life is all about, the nature of death, the purpose of suffering, and so on. It is only when we abandon the known in order to find the unknown, when we sacrifice the conscious for the unconscious, that we get nearer to those truths. For this we must use words in their nonfactual forms. Stories, poems, songs, and myths will tell us about the true nature of life.

Stories are about what happens to the personality as it shapes itself and is shaped by the inner and the outer world. Stories are metaphors for the struggles of the psyche, and they contain more important and more valuable information about how to live our lives than can be compiled on even the most sophisticated computer's database.

The Power of Words

hen words are used as representatives of the factual, linear world, they can be manipulated, rationalized, and categorized. They can be quickly understood and quickly forgotten. The factual description of a lake, for instance, could include the depth and flow of the water, its chemistry, temperature, and turbidity. The lake could be compared to others of its size or could be examined in terms of its geographic location. But it is only when it is described poetically that the image of the lake becomes vital. When words are used poetically they have the power to move us to laughter or to tears and give sense to our lives, and even to death.

We experience the world not verbally or consciously but through symbols, which are a spontaneous expression of the unconscious. Much of our existence remains on the irrational level, beyond the score of conscious understanding and beyond words used literally. A primary experience is the physical, emotional sensation that is only approximated by a word or a group of words. When we try to explain the color red or to describe something salty, for example, we must go beyond words, touching the imagination. This is because the body and the inner mind do not speak in the language of words.

The word itself, used in its metaphoric, poetic context, slowly sinks into our beings and affects our lives. When words are used to represent symbols and images, they carry messages from the silent but wise inner self, to be recognized and categorized by the logical left brain in terms of their relationship to other information. We use these words to express the most important episodes of our lives and to make sense of what happens. Often it is this use of words that makes the critical difference in a situation, and this is the value of learning to think, speak, and understand in symbolic, abstract terms.

When words are used by the conscious self, they have a great deal of power over the inner mind as well. What the unconscious hears, it believes without logic or qualification. The inner self listens passively and accepts as truth whatever we say to it. (This is why we often feel sick after we call the office to say we can't come to work due to illness, when we had actually just intended to take the day off.)

The words we use carry tremendous weight. If we say pessimistic, cynical things, the subconscious mind will listen and believe what we say. Even thinking words silently has that effect; the subconscious mind hears, believes, and acts on the words we think.

Our words are our messengers. The words we speak return to us, either as blessings or burdens. They become our experience. It is therefore important to speak words of strength and harmony, words to bring out the best in ourselves and in others.

In fact, just thinking positive thoughts about others seems to have a mysterious power. For example, it is often more beneficial to think positive thoughts about someone than to give them criticism or advice. When others perceive our positive thoughts on an intuitive and subconscious level, they feel encouraged to develop their own strengths. This is the secret to being a great teacher in the Socratic tradition. If you believe in the fundamental, innate understanding of the individual, educating becomes merely a process of stimulating and eliciting the individual's inner wisdom.

This, too, is the basis of positive thinking programs. The subconscious mind will endeavor to substantiate what we tell ourselves, believing that whatever it is told is factual. If we say we are sick, we will feel sick. If we say we feel strong, we will feel strong. The inner mind believes what it hears and acts accordingly.

Prayer is an example of the positive use of words. When we pray, we believe. Because we believe, our words have a powerful effect.

If we see a mental picture and use appropriate words, we can actually condition or brainwash our inner minds into assuming that the information we have given it is true. If we mentally see ourselves performing successfully, our subconscious mind will assume that we have done so and that we can do so again. This is why the basketball players in the experiment noted in chapter 4 were able to increase their scores just by imagining they had practiced. Whatever we want out of life must first be accepted by the inner mind, which silently controls our destinies.

If we see ourselves as attractive, healthy, and successful, and if we tell ourselves that picture is accurate, our inner minds will cooperate. If, on the other hand, we tell ourselves that we are fat, ugly losers, we will find our frame of mind corresponds to that image, and we will slouch through life, turning those negative images into fact. This is the power our words have over our lives. What we forecast, we become.

In addition, if the words we use come from deep within, as expressions of our mental pictures, they will carry the weight of destiny and manifest themselves as the future.

This is the experience symbolized by the figures falling from the Tower, trapped by their own limited perspective and finally pushed out into a reassessment, which gives them a chance to build new images for themselves and to transform their lives. The Tower represents false ideas. Lightning is breaking down existing forms of society and social interaction, or forms of communication, to make way for new ones, through a flash of insight from the subconscious.

The two figures falling to the ground have been devastated because they had limited themselves to external forms of experience. Lightning brings a breakthrough, reminding us that life can become full and rich when we allow ourselves to experience our feelings and sensations. We can overcome our limitations when we tell ourselves it is possible to do so.

What we say and think affects who we are. Words can heal us when they are used as messengers of the spirit. The two fallen figures are ready to rediscover the use of words as expressions of sensations and feelings, which will help integrate their experiences with their thoughts.

Looking at . . .

Mind over Body

The following biofeedback experiment is an illustration of the effect mental images can have on the body. For this exercise, you will need an ordinary room thermometer.

1. Take the temperature of the first two fingers of your right hand by pinching them together with a room thermometer between them.

2. Imagine that your hands are sitting in a bowl of ice water. Imagine this as vividly as you can. Mentally picture the ice and the way it feels on your fingers.

3. Take the temperature of your two fingers again. Continue to imagine that your fingers are in a bowl of ice water, until you actually see the temperature of your fingers drop.

From this demonstration, you will see the tremendous power your mind can exert over your body and thus over your life.

Step VI in Review

In Step VI you had a confrontation with the Devil. Write down the nature and definition of your own personal Devil and what that image has to teach you about your struggles at this point in your life. Write about your own prison, or Tower, and how that can be broken down in order to liberate you.

Write down the most important feeling and insights you have gained about yourself from the Devil. What is the best way to vanquish the Devil and escape from the Tower?

Step VII
Rebirth

The hero has died violently and visited the underworld.
Now is the time for rebirth and the defeat of death.

Seasons run in cycles, the sun and the moon have their
times. This is the season of rebirth; the demons have been
defeated and from the depths of your own psyche
you are ready to be born anew.

Chapter 18
The Star

he star represents inner vision; it is the eyes of the night. It is hope in the dark, the all-seeing eye, and the Queen of Heaven. The woman in the picture is reflecting upon elements of the universal, and upon the cosmic, as it is separated from the personal and the ego-centered concerns of everyday life.

Fishing

See yourself in a small boat, floating along a stream.

See yourself floating along in a small boat. You throw a line into the water. You pull something up.

What is it? _____

What color is it? _____

What does it look like? _____

How do you feel about it? _____

What do you do with it? _____

The object you pulled out of the water speaks to you. It says:

I am _____

I feel _____

I will _____

I think _____

I must _____

I secretly _____

You continue floating in your boat. How do you feel? _____

Where are you going? _____

What will you do when you get there? _____

Fishing represents becoming aware of unconscious attitudes, opinions, and feelings. The object you pulled out was from your unconscious mind.

This exercise can help you discover your deeper feelings and thoughts. It reflects your inner mind, or hidden side. If the creature you pulled up is ugly, frightening, or in any way menacing, stop here and have a further conversation with it. Ask it about the source of your discomfort and any other questions that seem important to you, and write down the answers. Later, go over these answers to get a clear picture of the problem. Accept whatever you find and discover ways to negotiate with it. In order to be happy and well, you need to develop new ways to get on good terms with your hidden side.

Down the stream is a symbol of the future. If you don't like what you see, visualize something better, and keep that image.

The fisherman is fishing for Neptune, the unconscious masculine part of the self, and for the mermaid, the unconscious feminine part of the self. Fishing is a common theme in dreams. It symbolizes becoming aware of unconscious feelings and attitudes.

The Star

No star is ever lost
We once have seen,
We always may be what
We might have been.

A. Procter
Legend of Provence

The star represents the step on our journey in which we will learn that all the experiences we have are necessary for the tempering of our characters.

Stars are often used to represent guiding forces. Mariners used them to find their way across uncharted seas. Astrologers use them to predict future trends. The star of Bethlehem guided the Magi to the manger.

The stars are the light by which our inner awareness is guided. Their message is that if we will listen, we will become illuminated; truth will unveil itself to us in the silence. Meditation is the art of listening in that silence.

The star is said to represent a
divine presence.

Meditation

We are usually only vaguely aware of our mental states. We only become aware of the way we feel when we are experiencing extreme emotions. When we do notice the way we feel, we usually assume that our mental state was produced by some outward event or circumstance beyond our control. We think we are the victims of chance;

we are ruled by the weather, other people, or luck. We believe we do not possess the power to control our own feelings.

But actually we do have the capability to control our thoughts and feelings. They originate inside us, not in someone's remarks or in the weather or in fate. And because they come from within us, we can control them. The easiest way to do this is by learning to meditate.

Meditation is the tool through which we can develop the ability to control our mental states. It is the practice of looking inward to overcome outward stimuli and develop a peaceful frame of mind. When we are inwardly at peace, we can tap that great wealth of power, the unconscious self, the source of all wisdom.

By meditating we can hold onto a positive outlook and protect ourselves from being swept into discouragement and despair. Meditation allows us to rid ourselves of the tensions, anxieties, and stresses that haunt us every day, by relaxing our bodies and cleansing our minds. Every minute of every day we receive constant random external stimuli. To sustain order and discover ourselves in the face of this continual assault, it is necessary to find an inner base, a center. Through the practice of meditation we can establish a communication with our inner selves, to find a part of ourselves that can remain impervious to the noise of the world.

Meditation is more than just a mental exercise, and more than a technique for seeking personal improvement. It is the experience of quietly receiving inspiration and illumination from within, by rising out of the realm of ordinary daily thought and entering into an idealized consciousness of intuitive thought. When we meditate, we are seeking the source of wisdom that lies within. This is the source that can provide all the answers and solutions to the daily demands of life.

The purpose of meditation is to learn to quiet the conscious mind, ignoring all the extraneous business and mental chatter the mind constantly occupies itself with, in order to quietly discover an inner, intuitive, creative self.

Many great inventors and scientists have said that their most brilliant solutions to frustrating problems did not come to them when they sat concentrating and struggling for answers. Instead, inspiration came after they had given up and gone out for a walk or decided to take a nap. The answers seemed to materialize from nowhere after all conscious analysis and examination had ceased. When we meditate, we are seeking that mental stillness that allows answers to emerge. All

The five-pointed star (pointed upward) represents aspirations, light, and spiritual guidance.

the trivia and the small talk of the conscious mind only serve to intrude upon the inner calm. In meditation we learn to allow distractions to float peacefully away, leaving the conscious mind open and quiet.

Using a force of will does not effectively silence the inner chatter, because that force itself is a conscious exertion and defeats the purpose. Instead, finding a state of mental quiet is a matter of putting aside all the noise and going deeper inside to a quiet place beyond words, the place of pure meaning.

Often we mistake the word for the thing itself, but the word is only a conscious effort to identify an inner truth. When the mind is using words it is not possible to find genuine significance, since all we can learn from words is what they approximately represent. The right brain speaks to us only through images, symbols, and feelings, so when the left side is chattering noisily, the right side cannot be heard. In meditation we are giving the creative, silent side a chance to communicate with us.

A person who is meditating will experience an inner stillness and calm as the mind focuses inward. However, there are no flashes of creative brilliance or dramatic sudden creative inspirations. The effects of meditation are usually subtle and gradual. The meditator simply feels more peaceful, poised, and in harmony with life. When the mind is clear, creative answers can flow in, because the meditator is tapping the realms of creative wisdom.

Meditating provides space for a new flow of ideas that will improve the way we feel, the way we respond to situations, and the quality of the work we do. Meditating opens up the inner reservoir of creativity, insights, ideas, and power, and makes them available for our daily use. It is a form of relaxation that releases inner resources for self-realization, psychic freedom, harmony, and creativity.

This is a form of mandala called a yantra, made of nine linked triangles. The mandala symbolizes wholeness and is often used as a visual point of concentration for meditation.

Looking at . . .

The Purposes of Meditation

The objective of meditation is to bring the soul into harmony and communion with the universe and with God, and to find the kingdom within.

Meditate to find a moment of quiet, away from the noise and confusion.

Meditate to retain a sense of self.

Meditate to find peace and harmony.

Meditate to keep a harmonious balance between yourself and your daily life.

Meditate in order to gain clarity and perspective.

Meditate in order to draw upon your own healing powers.

Meditate for guidance and direction.

Meditate in order to become infused with the spirit of God.

The kingdom of God is within you.
Jesus

Looking at . . .

How to Meditate

In order to be effective, meditation should be practiced at least once a day for about fifteen minutes at a time. First, read the directions below, and then go back and follow them step by step.

1. Choose a time a few hours after eating, since the digestive processes interfere with meditating. Sit in a comfortable chair in a quiet room. Make sure your clothing and shoes are loose enough so you can completely relax.

2. Sit back and let go of all thoughts, worries, and fears, and let yourself quietly relax.

3. Relax your hands on your lap and let your head lean slightly forward. Do not cross your legs. Close your eyes. Relax your body.

4. Beginning with an awareness of your feet, loosen the tension you find in them. Then work up to your ankles, then your calf muscles, and on up your leg, slowly relaxing your body one section at a time. When you reach your face, note the tension that collects in your forehead and around your mouth as you let go and relax the muscles. Mentally scan your body for tension. When you find a tense spot, let it go, and relax.

5. Most systems of meditation use a mantra, a word that serves as a broom to sweep all other thoughts out of your mind. The mantra becomes the only sound in your head, a part of your breathing. Pick a sound, like *om* or *amen*. (Herbert Benson, who wrote *The Relaxation Response*, uses the word *one*.) Continue repeating your mantra as you breathe.

6. Your breathing is important. You should take deep but natural breaths, using your diaphragm. Breathe in. Now, as you are breathing out, mentally say the word you have chosen as your mantra. Do this each time you breathe, letting all other words and thoughts fade away.

7. You should be breathing through your nose. Now try taking a deep breath and holding it for 15–20 seconds, then let it out slowly. Pause and repeat this several times, then return to normal breathing as you continue to meditate.

Every Human being is a cosmos with all the stars within.
Paracelsus

   Something like the effects of meditation takes place naturally when we do such things as gardening, sun-bathing, sailing, taking a walk, taking a ride, listening to music, and doing crafts, or any time when the conscious mind becomes relaxed and inner thoughts are allowed to come through.

   Meditation is an efficient way of relaxing oneself completely within a few minutes, to quiet the conscious mind and experience the stillness within, in order to leave room for deeper levels of inspiration and understanding.

When you have found the beginning of the way,
the star of your soul will show you its light.
The Kabbalah

*The nine-pointed star of three triangles is known as
the mystic star and is often used as a mandala.*

*The six-pointed star represents the creation and is
also the Seal of Solomon. It combines the
masculine and feminine triangles.*

Chapter 19
The Moon

e are like the moon. We cannot be contained within one definition. We are changeable and dynamic. There is nothing static about our human condition. Every day we look a little different and feel different than we did before. Like the moon, we change continually. Everything living is in a continual state of dynamic transformation.

True meaning is not suspended, available for exploration by mathematics or by physics, and we cannot understand the complexities and mysteries of life merely through calculations and abstractions. It is through intuition, from deep in the treasure vaults of the subconscious, that we can gain a true understanding of life.

Looking at . . .

The Moon

he full moon glistens over the lake. As you walk along the pathway past the towers, you can see with a clarity you have never had before. You hear a sound overhead, and as you glance toward the heavens, you can discern the face of a woman on the great round disc of the moon.

The woman in the moon is the eye of the night, the weaver of fate. It is she who controls the tides, rains, waters, floods, and the seasons. She is the bringer of change. The woman in the moon speaks to you. She says:

Be careful of _____

Your wisdom comes from _____

Always remember _____

Use your _____

The woman in the moon gives you this message: _____

_____

The moon represents your imagination and intuitive powers. The woman in the moon is the voice of these gifts. Your responses to this exercise come from your inner knowledge.

*The waters of life flow between the masculine sun of the conscious
mind, and the feminine moon of the unconscious.*

Say to yourself:
I am in tune with my inner wisdom, and my life is enriched by a wealth
of intuitive understanding and human insight.

We can go past immediate facts into a realm of timelessness where reality is fluid
and variable, and truth is unwavering. This is the goal we reach by the journey
into the primal night; this is the message of the moon.

Goddess of the Moon

 he beautiful Selene, goddess of the moon, glides through the night
sky pulling the moon behind her. She rides in a chariot drawn by
two oxen, whose horns are the image of the crescents of her gleam-
ing crown.

The goddess stops amid the flaming stars at the top of the sky, and the great orb of
the moon shines upon all the world, perfect for one night. Then, gradually, the moon
begins to fade. Night by night it shrinks until the world is covered in blackness.

Then the ruler of the darkness, the great Hecate, goddess of the underworld, arrives to rule the night. Hecate wears a nest of snakes in her long black hair. The snakes' skin is always being shed and renewed. Until the new moon appears in the sky, this dread queen of darkness reigns supreme. She is the ruler of the dark moon, of the world, and of the underworld.

Hecate's message is: Without darkness there can be no light, without death there can be no life.

Hecate, the goddess of the dark side of the moon, wore a nest of snakes in her hair.

The Grocer

 young grocer set out on his way to market to buy vegetables to sell in his shop. He had to leave home in the middle of the night in order to reach the market when it opened. On his way, he had a hunch that something good was going to happen to him. "This is going to be a lucky trip for me," he thought.

When the young grocer was halfway to market, he was surprised to find a sheaf of paper on the road. He picked it up. Only a sliver of a moon shone, and it was so dark that the grocer had to wait until sunrise to examine his find.

When it was sufficiently light to see, the grocer examined the packet. He was amazed to find that it contained fifteen hundred-dollar bills. He was so excited and delighted that he rushed to market and bought some lean meat, fresh fruit, and rice, and entirely forgot to buy fresh vegetables for his shop.

When the young man got home, his mother asked why he had no vegetables. He told her that he had found fifteen hundred-dollar bills on the road and when he got to the market he had bought food to eat but had entirely forgotten to buy the vegetables.

"Are you sure this money is not stolen?" his mother asked. "If you found it on the ground you must take it back! Go to the place where you found it and wait for the person who lost it to return. Then you can give it back to him."

So the vegetable grocer returned to the spot where he had found the money the night before. Soon a man came by and said he had lost his money. As he handed over the sheaf, the young grocer never thought to ask this man how much money he had lost. The bystanders who had gathered to watch urged the man to give the young grocer a reward for his honesty in returning the money, but the miserly man said, "I lost thirty hundred-dollar bills. Half of my money is missing."

A great argument developed among the bystanders over the amounts claimed. Finally the matter was taken to court. The judge questioned the young man and then his mother, and found their answers to be in agreement. He asked the two disputing parties to submit written statements to the court. The man swore that he had lost thirty hundred-dollar bills; the young grocer swore that he had found fifteen hundred-dollar bills.

Finally the judge made his decision. "The money that was found was not this man's money," he said. "The fifteen hundred-dollar bills will go to the worthy and honest young grocer and his mother." Then he told the man who said he had lost his money, "The thirty hundred-dollar bills you lost must be someplace else. Go and look for them yourself."

Reflections . . .

The Search for the Soul

editation is a technique that will enable the mind and body to become quiet so we can focus our attention on the inner self. Ironically, our search inward will ultimately lead us outward, past the self-centered preoccupations of the ego, to an openness with life.

If our entire focus were on ourselves, we would eventually reach a dead end. But when we go off in search of our souls, we are going beyond the self, looking for more meaning than the limits of the self can provide. When we go past the ego, we open our perceptions to a greater scheme of things.

Because all things are constantly in a state of change, it is often difficult to get our bearings if we are looking for external landmarks. But when we search within, the answers, although they are ever-changing, are always available to us.

Often when we find ourselves in a state of stupor, hopelessness, pain, loneliness, depression, and even madness, we may be on the verge of great vision and inspiration. Our condition of desperation is often only a stopping place on the road to greater self-development.

By looking inward, we can find a way past destruction, to salvation and to a new life. If we can learn to trust that a greater power than our own exists, and if we allow ourselves to go past our limitations, we will discover that we are capable of transcending the boundaries of the self and that we have a wealth of resources available to us. By using the power of faith to take us past the immediately obvious, into the realm beyond, we will find a place where life is constantly in a dynamic state of change and growth, and where our imagination is stronger than our will.

All things are changing, nothing dies. The spirit wanders, comes now here, now there, and occupies whatever form it pleases. For that which once existed is no more, and that which was not has come to be: and so the whole round of motion is gone through again.

Ovid

Entering the Belly of the Whale

he sun is always the same, always itself, never in any sense becoming. The moon, on the other hand, is a body that waxes and wanes and disappears, a body whose existence is subject to the universal law of becoming, of birth and death.

The moon, like man, has a career involving tragedy. The cycle of the moon's existence, like man's, ends in death. For three nights the starry sky is without a moon. But this death is followed by a rebirth, that of the new moon.[13]

The perpetual cycle of the moon returning to its beginnings makes the moon representative of the rhythms of life. It is related to the cycles of tides, rains, plant life, and fertility. The imagery associated with the moon's disappearance into the black night sky and reappearance is echoed in the story of Jonah and the whale, and in the various night sea journeys of mythology. In these stories the hero must overcome the monster that can devour the conscious mind.

In this case, entry into the belly of the monster is symbolized by the moon's disappearance into the sky, which, in psychological terms, is an emotional regression into the primal night. To come back out again is to pass from chaos to creation.

It is often necessary for us to experience some kind of mental chaos before we can have a psychic renewal. Therefore, there is no advantage in avoiding emotional upheaval. What we need to do is to learn how to go through the pilgrimage into the dark. There we will find something valuable about ourselves and about our lives, which we can take back with us when we return home from our journey of the soul.

Expressed in symbolic terms, the moon represents the intuitive understandings that we can find within ourselves. We may need to make a trip down into the cosmic waters to capture them, or to experience a time of emotional turbulence and depression, but we can always find our way back from the darkness, to emerge as the new moon, ready to begin again the cycle of life and growth.

Chapter 20
The Sun

he sun represents the universal life force; it is the symbol of supreme cosmic power. It is the center of being and intelligence, the eye of the world. Dante said, "There is no visible thing in all the world more worthy to serve as a symbol of God than the sun, which illuminates with visible light, first itself, then all the celestial and mundane bodies."

The child in this picture represents the person who has undergone the trials and symbolic deaths of life, which transform us into fuller, wiser, more holy human beings. The sunflowers show a turning away from the negative, toward the light.

In many of the world's myths the sun is seen as the midpoint in the sky, the door through which souls pass back from time into eternity.

Looking at . . .

The Power of the Sun

he heat of the sun warms you as you walk along the overgrown path. You feel its power as it seeps into the deepest fibers of your being. Your mind is clear. You are inspired. You now understand things that have eluded you in the past. The sun shines on the secret places and reveals hidden answers, and you are enlightened.

New wisdom and great powers of comprehension tell you that:

You can _____

You have _____

You will _____

You understand _____

You are now able to _____

You can achieve _____

The sun represents enlightenment and understanding. The gifts of the sun are clarity and wisdom. The energy of the sun is a symbol for personal growth, optimism, and idealism. The circle of the sun represents wholeness and creativity.

Say to yourself:
I am enthusiastic and optimistic. I have a sense of clarity and understanding, and I look forward to a time of creativity and personal growth.

The sun represents the all-seeing divinity and the center of being, where intuitive understanding is found.

Looking at . . .

Exercise of the Sun

This exercise will give you an idea of your feelings about yourself and how you can improve them.

On the spokes of the circle below, write down all the things you dislike or believe to be faults about someone you know. Inside the circle, write down all the opposites to those faults. After you have written down everything you can think of on the outside of the circle and the opposites inside, cut out the circle.

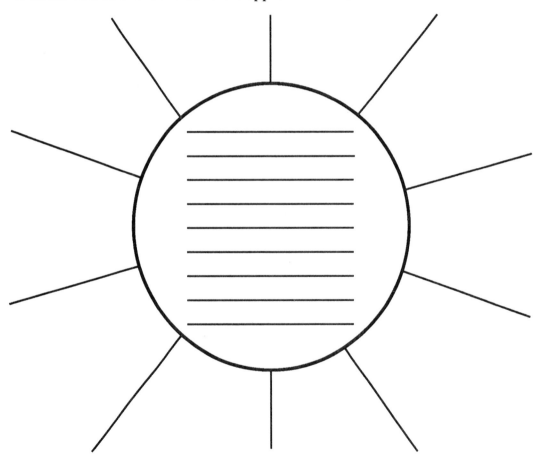

What you have left will be a circle that contains all of your own desired attributes. The faults you listed on the outside are those you believe are your own. Their opposites, on the inside of the circle, are the qualities you esteem.

Tape this circle to your bathroom mirror and read it aloud every day, beginning with the words, "I am . . ."

Looking at . . .

The Banner and the Rainbow

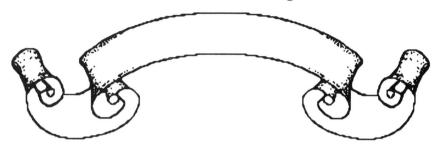

The child on the white horse carries a banner in her left hand.

What color is the banner? _____

There is a message on the banner. What does it say? _____

There is a rainbow in the sky with a message on it. What does it say? _____

_____

_____

The banner represents victory over darkness. The color you chose for the banner reflects your feelings about the nature of this victory. (Look up its symbolism in the color index.) The rainbow is a sign of glory, happiness, and protection to come in the future.

The sun represents the conscious mind. When it is awakened to our hidden motives, we can set about correcting and changing our negative habits and thoughts into positive ones.

Looking at . . .

Positive Visualization

he secret to good health and happiness is to learn to combat stress or the undermining forces (call them bad luck, evil, or whatever) of life. Positive visualization is one of the most effective means of overcoming negative mental programs. Try the following exercise for creating new, positive mental programs.

Write down a situation that has been bothering you.

_____

1. Meditate until you feel peacefully relaxed.

2. Imagine the best possible solution to the situation you wrote down. This should be a solution that fulfills your fondest dreams. Imagine this solution in clear detail; see the whole picture, with yourself in the middle. Dwell on this picture for five to ten minutes.

3. Now, whenever this situation starts to bother you, immediately picture yourself in your dream solution, until it becomes as familiar and real to you as the problem itself has been.

> When your visualized solution is the prevailing image in your mind, it will gradually become the reality, as you progress toward your goal.

Hymn to Ra

The ancient Egyptians expressed their reverence toward the sun. In the following hymn to Ra—god of the sun, symbol of light, illumination, and spiritual awakening.

Ra, the god of the sun

Homage to you, O sun, when you riseth as a god. You are adored by me when your beauties are before my eyes and when your radiance falls upon my body. You go forth to your setting in your boat with the fair winds and your heart is glad; the heart of the morning boat of the sun rejoices as you stride over the heavens in peace; and all your foes of darkness are cast down. The never-resting stars sing hymns which never fail to glorify you as you sink to rest in the horizons of the mountains of sunset. O you who are beautiful at morn and at eve. Hail you disk of rays who rises on the horizons day by day! Shine with your beams of light upon the world.

Egyptian Book of the Dead

Egyptian sundial

Light Supreme

he rays of the sun symbolize the transmission of divine energy to the world. Divine energy is said to continuously circulate through the sun door; God descends and mankind ascends through the doorway of the Sun.

Dante describes his feelings of exultation and reverence toward the light, that is, the sun or spiritual illumination, in the following poem.

O light supreme, that art so far exalted
Above our mortal ken! Lend to my mind
A little part of what thou dist appear,
And grant sufficient power unto my tongue
That it may bare for races yet unborn,
At least one spark for thy almighty flame!
For if thou wilt come back to my remembrance,
That I may sing thy glory in these lines,
The more thy victory will be explained.
I think the brightness of the living ray
That I endured would have bewildered me
If once my eyes had turned aside from it.
And I recall that for that very reason
I was emboldened to endure so much
Until my gaze was joined unto His good,
Abundant grace, by which I could presume
To fix my eyes upon the Eternal Light
Sufficiently to see the whole of it![14]

The sun is the eating bowl of God, an inexhaustible grail, abundant with the substance of the sacrifice, whose flesh is meat indeed and whose blood is drink indeed.

Joseph Campbell
The Hero with a Thousand Faces

The Baker's Daughter

here was once a baker who had two daughters. Although they were twins, they were as different as could be. One was cheerful, generous, and good-natured, while the other was suspicious, selfish, greedy, and cross.

One cold evening while the wind whipped through the icy streets, the good-natured sister was working in her father's bakery. An old woman in ragged clothes came in from the cold and asked the girl if she might have a tiny bit of dough.

"Of course," answered the girl.

"And may I bake it in your oven?" the old woman asked.

"Of course," the girl responded.

The old woman found a place in the corner of the shop and sat there napping

254

while her dough baked. Then the girl called out to her, "Wake up, wake up, old woman, your dough has doubled in size!"

"And thus it shall ever be for you, my child, because of your generous heart," answered the old woman, who threw off her ragged cloak and suddenly became a shining princess. She touched the girl with her magic wand, and then she vanished from sight. From that day on, everything the girl put into the oven came out twice the size it had been.

Time passed. One cold winter's evening the ill-natured daughter was tending the bakery. An old woman dressed in rags entered the shop and asked the girl, "Might I have a tiny bit of dough?" The girl hated to waste good dough on an old beggar woman, but she finally consented because her father had told her not to refuse bread to beggars.

"And will you bake it for me?" the old woman asked.

"Oh, all right," the girl agreed grudgingly.

The old woman sat in the corner of the shop napping while she waited for her bread. But when the baker's daughter saw that the dough had doubled in size, she grumbled to herself, "This is too much bread to give to an old beggar woman," and she set the big loaf aside for herself. She took an even smaller piece of dough and put it in the oven for the old woman.

When the bread was done, the girl opened the oven door and found that it had become even larger than the first loaf. "I will not waste this fine loaf on that nasty old beggar," she thought, as she put the bread aside for herself. Then she took an even smaller pinch of dough and put it into the oven. But when she took it out of the oven she found it had become a big, wonderful loaf of bread filled with fruits, nuts, and spices.

"This is far too good to give to an old beggar!" she thought, and she ate the whole loaf herself. Then she woke the old woman and said, "There is no bread for you, your loaf burned and we have no more to spare."

"Is that all you have to say?" asked the old woman. The girl only laughed at her in scorn and sent her out of the bakery.

"Then that is how it shall ever be for you," replied the old woman, who threw off her ragged cloak and became a shining princess. She touched the girl with her magic wand, and forever after whatever the girl put into the oven was burned.

This fable illustrates the consequences of the choices we make. The generous twin was able to see her fortunes double, while the selfish twin got back nothing in return for her selfishness.

A Positive Attitude

ad luck is often nothing more than a negative attitude toward life. Our beliefs determine our experiences; our ideas and thoughts are the seeds of our speech and action. The way we feel depends on our frame of mind, and that alters our perceptions of the world. Even when we think we are really responding to the way life is treating us, we are in fact merely reacting to the way we feel about life.

When we do respond to external stimuli, it is we ourselves who determine what we will respond to and how we will respond to it. For example, we can train ourselves to respond only to positive stimuli and ignore the rest. Usually, however, we do just the opposite. We focus on every hint that implies we are not good enough, and we forget all our successes.

Most of us have become so accustomed to the idea that it is inappropriate for us to be successful that we block out positive opportunities and experiences, harboring only the negative ones. We have become accustomed to expect the negative in life, so we interpret each experience negatively. This only serves to reinforce our negative expectations of future experiences, so we go around and around in a self-defeating, self-perpetuating cycle, creating our own bad luck, like the selfish twin in the story.

However, we do have choices. Misery is optional, not inevitable. We can change our insidious mental patterns by retraining ourselves.

Positive Mental Programming

ositive mental programming is a little like dieting, except that in mental programming you have to become aware of the thoughts you think instead of the foods you eat. Reprogramming the mind requires that you become aware of your negative thoughts, negative words, and destructive actions. In order to change your thinking, whenever you hear yourself think a negative thought, you immediately replace it with its opposite, positive thought. As soon as a negative word begins to form in your mind, you replace it with its opposite, positive word. You change every destructive action into a beneficial one.

Although this may seem awkward at first, it soon becomes a habit to think, speak, and act positively. Then, as a result of learning to control your mental habits, your potentially negative experiences can be converted into positive ones, and bad luck can become transformed into good.

The sun and the lion represent strength and courage to overcome the demon. Negative experiences can be converted into positive ones by controlling negative thoughts.

Being Successful

he successes we will have in the future are based on our sense of confidence from past successes. This confidence puts us into a relaxed frame of mind to let success happen automatically. Therefore, all we need is to keep past successes in mind and forget about anything else. A failure serves simply to teach us how not to do something. Once we have learned that lesson, we should forget the failure, because if we carry it around it will influence our future behavior.

We cannot consciously command ourselves to be successful any more than we can command ourselves to relax. However, we can consciously decide to feel successful. We can decide that we want to be physically and mentally healthy, and we can achieve that goal by predisposing our unconscious minds to positive, successful outlooks.

What goes on in the mind affects the body's responses. Thus our actions, feelings, and behavior are often the results of our mental condition. If we change our mental images, we can automatically change our actions, feelings, and behavior. We behave in accordance with what we imagine. The key to success is to control our mental images. Anything we want to change must begin with the way we think.

We are usually the victims of habit. We expect whatever we are used to. However, since it is possible to control our mental images through simple exercises, we can gain control of our imagination. We always carry the outline of our lives in the form of our beliefs about ourselves. Once that outline is changed, we will change.

Hypnosis is an example of the power of mental images. Under hypnosis, your unconscious mind can be told that you are holding a hot coal, and your fingers may actually blister, even if you are holding nothing. On the other hand, Indian yogis can walk on hot coals without feeling the heat, because they have learned to control their mental processes. The mental image can be stronger than external fact.

If you can imagine yourself being successful, you will find a successful path. Imagine yourself healthy, and your body will heal itself. Imagine yourself happy, and that is the way you will feel. At every moment you can direct your own life; you are in charge of your own destiny.

The secret to good health is to learn to overcome the stress that makes us susceptible to disease. The secret to happiness is to learn to overcome the negative forces that make us susceptible to adversity. We can change our fate by changing our attitude.

Developing Positive Thought Patterns

Use a small pocket notebook to write down all the negative ideas, remarks, and actions you make throughout the day. Whenever you hear yourself say, think, or do something negative, write it down. Then write down the opposite response in the next column.

For example,
if you hear yourself say: Change your words to:

I'm sorry I can't meet you.............................Sure, let's get together.

I'm getting too old...I'm at a good point in my life.

I'm getting too fat..I'm starting to diet and I feel good.

I don't feel like work today............................I feel good about work today.

It is very simple to say no or "I can't." It takes more energy to try than to give up. We are all lazy. Once we decide to try, however, we find that we possess a new kind of energy. Once we ignore the limitations of the conscious self that habitually thinks we cannot do something, we can surpass old limits and discover new abilities. This is a matter of developing a new kind of faith, a faith in ourselves and in our capabilities, which go far beyond our habitual expectations.

Life is a continual process of growth, change, and healing. Nature has a marvelous capacity for regeneration, and we ourselves have wonderful powers for self-healing. This does not happen self-consciously. We do not command ourselves to grow or change. Our growth and regeneration takes place unconsciously, and it happens best when our attitude toward life and toward ourselves is positive.

When you become aware of your thought patterns,
you can learn to turn negative thoughts into positive ones.

[Helios is the god of the sun who] plumbs all hearts, the infallible whom neither mortals nor immortals can deceive, either by action or in their most secret thoughts.

Pindar

*In this illustration, the moon is in the shadow of the earth,
or the psyche is in its deepest state of depression.
This is the point at which the new personality,
represented here by the sun, can be born.*

Step VII in Review

In Step VII you encountered the star, the moon, and the sun. They offered you messages about the pattern of meaning in your life and a richer understanding of who you are and where you are going. They are the source of your rebirth, based on self-understanding, self-development, and self-acceptance. Write a brief summary of the most important aspects of your rebirth.

Write down the most important feelings and insights you have gained about your rebirth.

Step VIII
Transformation

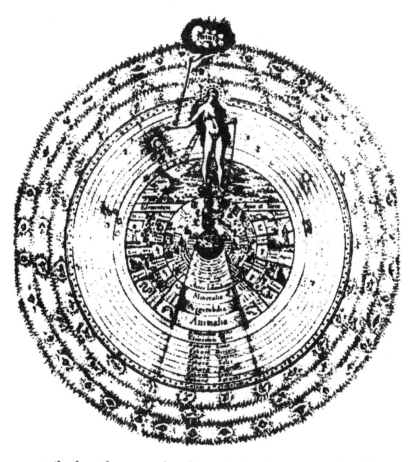

The hero has completed a cycle in the process of self-
realization that leads to freedom from fears and all
limitations, and to harmony with life. This is the final
event in the achievement of the self, which has lost all its
illusions of separation from life. This is the culmination of
the process of losing the self in order to find the self. You
have achieved a mythological consciousness, in which
the divine is active in all things and events.

Chapter 21
Judgment

he symbol of Judgment represents the regeneration of the psyche or the soul. After we have overcome the death of the spirit we will be capable of experiencing a psychological resurrection.

The people in the picture below are survivors of the lightning that struck them when they were in the Tower (see chapter 17).

Looking at . . .

The Angel of Judgment

An angel blowing her trumpet appears from a cloud in a winter sky. All over the world men, women, and children rise from their graves and stretch out their arms to the angel.

As you undergo a sense of personal redemption and regeneration, you are filled with a deep understanding of yourself and your life. You say to the angel:

My experience of inner death occurred when _____

because _____

I learned from it that _____

And now, in order to become resurrected, I must _____

I can now _____

I have to _____

I understand that _____

In the future, I will _____

I am _____

The angel represents the messenger who awakens in you a new realization. Angels are the messengers of God, bringers of enlightenment. The angel heralds your psychic rebirth, a resurrection and a renewed understanding of yourself and your life.

You have reached the plateau. Now you are ready to advance, to find a higher purpose and deeper meaning.

Lo! I tell you a mystery. We shall not all sleep, but we shall all be changed, in a moment, in the twinkling of an eye, at the last trumpet. For the trumpet will sound, and the dead will be raised imperishable, and we shall be changed. For this perishable nature must put on the imperishable, and this mortal nature must put on immortality.

1 Cor. 15:51–53

Say to yourself:
I respond to the call of the angel and the awakening of my soul.
I have a new sense of life and of purpose.

The Message

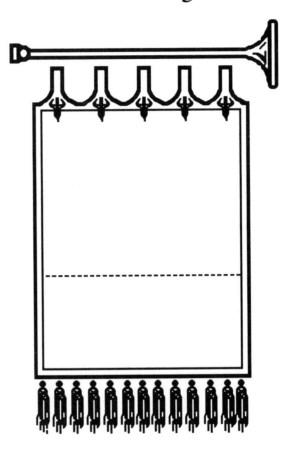

In the banner above, write a word that best expresses the essence of your personal sense of transformation.

Use this word as your mantra. Repeat it to yourself whenever you are depressed or have doubts about yourself and your direction.

Then I saw a new heaven and a new earth; for the first heaven and the first earth had passed away, and the sea was no more. And I saw the holy city, New Jerusalem, coming down out of heaven from God, prepared as a bride adorned for her husband; and I heard a loud voice from the throne saying, "Behold, the dwelling of God is with men. He will dwell with them, and they shall be his people, and God himself will be with them; he will wipe away every tear from their eyes, and death shall be no more, neither shall there be mourning nor crying nor pain any more, for the former things have passed away."

Rev. 21:1–4

Struck by Lightning

ircea Eliade says that a person who has survived being struck by lightning acquires a new sensibility unattainable through ordinary experience. With the destruction of all previous structures in his life, the person is forced to change. He comes to feel not only that he has died and been reborn, but that he has been born into a new world that looks like our ordinary world but has an added dimension. In terms of the ideas of the shaman or the medicine man in primitive cultures, this experience is often expressed as the combustion of the flesh and the breaking up of the skeleton.

Eliade tells the story of the Yakut, Bukes Ullejeen, who was struck by lightning and scattered into a thousand fragments.

> His friend hurried to the nearest village where he found several men who went back with him to collect the remains for burial. When they arrived at the site where Bukes was left, the men found him safe and sound. He said to them, "The God of Thunder came down from heaven and cut me into little pieces and now I have come back to life a shaman and I can see all around at a distance of thirty versts."[15]

In an instant Bukes had passed through the initiatory experience of psychic rebirth, which for most of us takes a long time, perhaps a lifetime.

The Gospel According to Saint Thomas makes reference to this kind of judgment and rebirth that takes place within the psyche:

> His disciples said to him: "When will the kingdom come?" Jesus said, "It will not come by expectation; they will not say: `See here,' or `See there.' But the kingdom of the Father is spread upon the earth and men do not see it."[16]

The Peasant Girl and the Judge

nce there were two peasants. One was well-off and the other was very poor. They were digging together in a field and they found a golden cup. "It is mine," said one. "No, it's mine," shouted the other. Finally the two agreed to seek the opinion of a judge.

The judge of the county was a young and rather arrogant man who was new to his job. Puzzled by the case, he decided to test the men with riddles. Whoever could come up with the best answer would be awarded the cup. These were the riddles the judge posed:

"What is the richest thing in the world?"

"What is the heaviest thing in the world?"

"What is the swiftest thing in the world?"

The well-off peasant went home and told his wife about the riddles. "Oh, I know the answers," his wife said. "The richest thing in the world is the king, the heaviest thing in the world is iron, and the swiftest thing in the world is our bay mare; she can outrun any horse in the country."

The other peasant was a poor widower who had a clever and loving daughter named Manka. He went home and told Manka the riddles. She said, "Tell the judge that the richest thing is the earth because she brings all that we need in this world. The heaviest thing is sorrow that weighs on our hearts. The swiftest thing is the mind, which can go to China and back in a moment."

When the peasants appeared before the judge and he heard their answers, he awarded the gold cup to the poor peasant. "Where did you find these answers?" he asked the old man.

The poor peasant replied, "Manka, my daughter, who is very wise for her years, told me what to say."

"I would like to meet this Manka," the judge said. "Please ask her to meet me at the court tomorrow."

When Manka and her father arrived at court the next day, they saw two brothers who were disputing the settlement of their father's land. However it was split, both argued that they did not get a fair portion.

The young judge greeted Manka and said to her, "Since you are so wise, tell me how you would decide this case." Manka said, "Have one brother divide the property, and the other brother can take first choice."

The two brothers were satisfied with this decision and the case was settled.

The judge smiled at Manka, thinking she was as pretty as she was clever. "I would like to marry your daughter," he told the old peasant. Manka agreed to marry the young judge, but when his family learned of the arrangements, they became very upset because Manka was a poor peasant girl.

Finally the judge sent word to Manka that he would marry her only if she would come to the wedding neither clothed nor naked, neither riding nor walking, and neither with a wedding gift nor without one.

When her father heard this he said, "Alas, poor Manka, I fear the judge and you will not be wed."

"Do not worry, father," Manka said. "I will go to market and find what I need." When she returned, she had a fishing net, which she wrapped around herself so that she was neither clothed nor naked. Then she saddled the old goat and mounted him,

270

and she put a pigeon under her arm and set off. As she traveled, her feet dragged along the ground so she was neither riding nor walking.

When the judge came out to meet her, she handed him the pigeon, which flew away as soon as he reached for it. "Here is your wedding gift," she told him. The judge laughed and said to Manka, "You have done as I asked and you shall be my bride. But you must promise never to interfere with my judgment at court."

So Manka and the judge were married. Soon two peasants came to court with a dispute. They had been hauling their goods to market when one man's mare had given birth to her foal under the other man's cart. Both men claimed ownership of the foal. The judge decided that the foal should go to the man under whose cart it had been born, saying, "Where the beast was born, there let it remain."

The peasant who owned the mare was very unhappy. He went to Manka, whom he had heard was very wise and just. At first she refused to interfere, but finally she agreed to help him, if he agreed not to give her away.

The next day, following Manka's instructions, the peasant brought a pail of water and a fishing rod to the road where the judge would pass on his way to court. When the judge saw the peasant, he asked, "What are you doing with a fishing pole in the middle of the road?"

"I am fishing," the man replied.

"But you can't catch fish in a bucket of water on the road," the judge said.

"Well, I have as much chance of catching a fish in a bucket as there is of a cart giving birth to a foal," he replied.

The judge agreed that he had been wrong in his decision. "You may take back your foal," he said. But first he made the peasant tell him who had helped him. The peasant confessed that it had been Manka.

The judge was furious with his wife. He told her that she must go back to her father's house since she had broken her promise to him. She agreed to go, but she asked him if she might take whatever she loved best with her from the house. The judge said she could take whatever she wanted.

Manka told her husband she would serve him a last dinner before she left. While she was preparing the meal, Manka put a sleeping potion in the judge's food. Then while he slept, she had the servants drive him to her father's house and put him to bed there.

The next morning when the judge awoke, he did not know where he was. He yelled out and Manka came into the little room where he slept. "You told me I might take whatever I loved most from your house, so I have taken you," she said.

The judge laughed and hugged her and said, "Manka, you are wiser than I. From now on we will sit in court and give our judgments together."

In the story of the peasant girl and the judge, human thoughts and feelings are shown to be of greater value than worldly goods, and the clever, nonliteral wisdom of the young woman (or of the inner self) is sounder than the literal pronouncements of the judge. Just when all appears to be lost, this intuitive wisdom can take us past the barriers and guide us to creative solutions and new realms of opportunity.

Reflections . . .

Setting Goals

e go where we dream of going. And the best way to go in a direction that will provide us with happiness and satisfaction is to make our dreams real by turning them into goals. If we believe in our goals and in ourselves, we can achieve anything we set out for.

We must, of course, be willing to take responsibility for all the work that goes into the accomplishment of our goals. We must have the self-control and self-discipline to do the job that makes our dreams possible. But it is in setting our goals that we will set the stage for the labor that transforms our dreams into reality.

When we define our goals, life suddenly takes shape and becomes meaningful. The prospect of meeting our goals gives us a sense of excitement and of direction.

When we are without goals, we often feel that life is beyond our control and that we are forced to take whatever falls our way. Then we feel disappointed and short-changed with our fate. To console ourselves we may overeat, drink, smoke, and spend our time seeking thrills to relieve our frustration. Or we may spend our time looking for someone else to blame for our failures. As a result, we feel we are going nowhere, so we have another drink, or another pill, or another doughnut, and the cycle begins all over again.

This negative cycle is broken only when we can discover our real goals, those goals that come to us from within. These goals are not for the benefit of others, to impress friends or gain their envy, admiration, or respect. To give us personal satisfaction, our goals must be personal; they must have a significance for us without regard to what other people think. For example, buying a boat or an airplane may seem to be a good goal, but these are just things, the materials of the outer world. They have no true significance or meaning in the inner world.

It is in discovering and pursuing our inner goals that we will find true satisfaction and fulfillment. In the process, we may be able to meet our material goals as well.

Sometimes it may seem tempting to leave the future to chance or to luck, but random chance cannot possibly take us where we want to go. It is our inner goals that can lead us to our own proper path. When we find it, that path will provide our every experience with a sense of content and of meaning.

Most of us function at only a small portion of our abilities to live rich, loving, caring, creative, and full lives. Meeting our potentials can become life's most exciting adventure.

We can find out about ourselves and our dreams simply by reaching inward, where we will discover the true nature of our feelings and desires. When we look within, we will gain the courage and the faith we need to embark upon our true path. When we see our inner goals clearly, we can move forward toward them, and in meeting these goals we will become regenerated.

Change and development take place when a person has risked himself and dares to become involved with experimenting with his own life.

Herbert Otto

The angel is the messenger of God, the symbol of enlightenment.

Looking at . . .

Setting Goals to Reach Your Objectives in Life

1. Meditate for at least ten minutes.

2. In a relaxed mental and physical state, put yourself into a positive frame of mind by saying to yourself, "I believe that all things are possible."

Look at the diagram below. In the first column, list four things in your life right now that you believe should be improved. In the second column, write how each item listed should be changed in three months. In the third column, list how the situation should be improved in a year. In the fourth column, list the changes that should take place in three years' time. In the last column, write the final solution to the problem, an outcome that would be entirely to your satisfaction.

This will give you a chart for your future. Refer to it whenever you find yourself feeling discouraged or confused about your objectives.

1 Things in my life right now to improve	2 Improvements to make in the next 3 months	3 Improvements to make in the next year	4 Improvements over the next 3 years	5 Ultimate ideal outcome

Chapter 22
The World

he image of the world represents the realized self in which the opposing forces of science and magic, spirit and flesh, mother and father, are united into one being. The conscious and unconscious, the instinct and the spirit all flow together.

The picture below depicts the dance of life, in which all of these elements constantly shift and merge in the kaleidoscope of existence.

Looking at . . .

The Dance of the World

One truly lives only when one dances.

Isadora Duncan

he woman who is dancing the square dance of the circle says to you:

I dance the dance of life, the pivot and the source of the cosmos.

Let me show you _____

I can help you _____

I will tell you _____

I will give you _____

She invites you to join in the dance. As you twirl and glide, she says:

You are _____

You have _____

There is a life force, an energy that is translated through you into action. And because there is only one you in all time, this expression is unique . . . It is not your business to determine how good it is, nor how valuable, nor how it compares with other expressions. It is your business to keep it yours clearly and directly, to keep the channel open.

Martha Graham

The dancer is the foundation, the source. She is mother nature. The dance represents the complexity of nature. In the dance you are freeing yourself of your limitations and taking charge of every aspect of your life.

Your responses indicate your areas of growth and your gifts. What does the dancer show you and tell you? Consider what she gives you. Your response to "You are" indicates your attributes, and to "You have," your gifts.

This illustration represents the world in terms of the mother as the creator.

Say to yourself:
I am a child of the universe. I am secure and sure of my place
in the scheme of things. All my needs are provided.

Looking at . . .

Squaring the Circle

Draw a picture using the circle below.

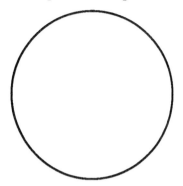

What is the title of your picture?

_____

How do you feel about the object you drew?

_____

Draw a picture using the square below.

What is the title of your picture?

_____

How do you feel about the object you drew?

_____

Draw a picture using the figure of the circle and square below.

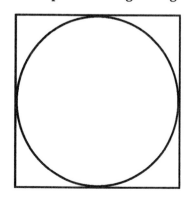

What is the title of your picture?

_____

How do you feel about the object you drew?

_____

The circle represents wholeness and eternity. It is completion and fulfillment. The square represents the earthly realm. Each corner stands for one of the four earthly elements: earth, air, fire, water.

Squaring the circle means unifying the heavenly with the earthly, or bringing heaven down to earth; it represents finding the sacred in the human experience.

The pictures you made out of these shapes express your feelings about them. See if you can find a relationship between the images you drew and your own feelings. The picture you drew from the circle is your image of wholeness; the picture from the square is your material side; and the squaring of the circle is your image of the sacred in your daily life.

Squaring the circle represents unifying the elements of heaven with the elements of the earth, or finding the sacred in the human experience.

The Wonders of the Universe

In the last canto of *The Divine Comedy*, Dante expresses his sense of the wonder of the universe that results from the unification of opposites.

I saw that in its depths there are enclosed,
Bound up with love in one eternal book,
The scattered leaves of all the universe—
Substance, and the accidents, and their relations,
As though together fused in such a way
That what I speak of is a single light
The universal form of this commingling
I think I saw, for when I tell of it
I feel that I rejoice so much the more.
One moment brought me more oblivion
Than five and twenty centuries could cast
Upon those Argonauts whose shadow once
Made Neptune wonder. Even thus my mind,
Enraptured, gazed attentive, motionless,
And grew the more enkindled as it gazed.

For in the presence of those radiant beams
One is so changed, that 'tis impossible
To turn from it to any other sight—
Because the good, the object of the will,
Is all collected there. Outside of it
That is defective which is perfect there.
Henceforth my speech will fall still further short
Of what I recollect as t'were a babe's
Wetting his tongue upon his mother's breast.

There was no other than a single semblance
Within that loving light on which I gazed,
For it is ever as it was before,
And yet by reason of my vision's power,
Which waxed the stronger in me as I looked,
That semblance seemed to change and I was well.

For within the substance, deep and radiant,
Of that High light, three circles showed themselves
Of one dimension, yet of triple hue.

One seemed to be reflected by the next,
As Iris by Iris, and the third
Seemed fire, shed forth equally by both.
How powerless is speech—how weak, compared
To my conception which itself is trifling
Beside the mighty vision that I saw!

O Light Eternal, that in thyself alone
Thou only know'st thyself, and in thyself
Both know and knowing, smilest on thyself!
That very circle which appeared in thee,
Conceived as but a reflection of a light,
When I had gazed on it awhile, now seemed
To bear the image of a human face
Within itself, of its own coloring—
Wherefore my sight was wholly fixed on it.
Like a geometer, who will attempt
With all his power and mind to square the circle,
Yet cannot find the principles he needs:
Just so was I, at that phenomenon.
I wished to see how image joined to ring.
And how the one found place within the other.
Too feeble for such flights were my own wings,
But by a lightning flash my mind was struck—
And thus came the fulfillment of my wish.

My power now failed that fantasy sublime:
Will and my desire were both revolved
As is a wheel in even motion driven,
By love, which moves the sun and every star.[17]

On the tree of knowledge, the branches are the sun, the moon, and the planets.
Above, the top triangle represents the soul, the spirit, and the body of the universe.
The triangle below is reversed, representing man's threefold essence.

Looking at . . .

The Tree of Life

magine that you sink your toes deep into the rich soil; your roots are strong and they nourish you. You grow tall and your great roots spread long and far under the ground. You spread your wonderful branches wide, reaching for the sun, and you revel in the deep nourishment you receive from the earth and the sun as you stretch heavenward.

From the nourishing bounty of the earth and the powerful energy of the sun you produce a magnificent fruit.

This fruit is _____

for _____

and with it you will _____

The seeds of this fruit will be _____

The tree is also often related to the Great Mother.

The tree in this exercise is your own internal synthesis of heaven and earth, conscious and subconscious capabilities. The fruit is the culmination of one state, the here and now, and the seeds of the next, the future. This exercise will indicate the direction in which you are growing.

The tree represents the whole world. Its roots grow into the earth or down into the underworld, tapping its waters in order to draw upon their powers. The trunk grows up into the realms of time. The branches spread out, representing the world of form. They grow toward heaven, reaching for the realms of the divine.

The Tree of Life

The tree has been a part of the myths, legends, and folklore of cultures all around the world throughout history. In ancient Egypt, the sycamore fig tree represented perpetual renewal in the afterworld. Oak trees were called the first mothers by the ancient Greeks and Romans, who believed these trees produced the first people. In Greek mythology, Adonis, the god of vegetation, was born from the trunk of a myrrh tree. Daphne changed into a laurel tree to escape from the god Apollo.

Hindus revere the banyan tree. The Buddha sat under the tree of enlightenment, the bhodi tree, which represents endless regeneration of the cosmos from a single transcendent source. Mohammed is said to have ascended through the seven planetary spheres to paradise by means of a tree. Christ and Buddha both rose to heaven along the symbolic center of the world, or the Tree of Life. And in many tribal cultures, the shaman climbs a symbolic mystical tree to reach the divine.

In Kundalini Yoga, the human spine is called the spinal tree, up which the serpent Kundalini is persuaded to ascend, piercing the various spiritual centers, or chakras, on its way, until it is released from the thousand-petaled lotus at the top of the head.

The ancient Egyptian celestial tree symbolizes perpetual renewal in the afterworld.

In Kundalini Yoga, the spinal column is the axis mundi, *or the spinal tree at the center of the universe.*

In the Bible, the cross on which Christ died was symbolically linked with the Tree of Life, which grew in the Garden of Eden and offered eternal life. In Judaism, the Tree of Life is most often represented by the flowering almond tree, which in the Near East heralds spring with fragrant white blossoms. Moses was instructed to make the cups, capitals, and flowers of the seven-branched candlestick, the menorah, in the pattern of the almond tree.

The menorah is related in both structure and symbolism to the model of the sacred tree in the ancient Near East.

The Tree at the Center of the Universe

 n the ancient world, the tree was worshipped as the *axis mundi*, the center of the universe. For the ancients, the tree seemed to join the three realms—the underworld, the earth, and the realms of the divine—and it made communication possible among the three. The tree represented the center of the universe, the point around which the world revolves.

This Scandinavian Tree of Life, the Yggdrasil, grows from the underworld, up through the world of men and then out into the realms of the gods.

All over the world, the tree represents the sacred tree or the cosmic tree. The alchemists called it the Tree of Life, from which the universe itself was said to grow. Through all the ages, this has been an image of the endless renewal of the cosmos from a single point; power is said to radiate throughout the world from the cosmic center of the universe. The tree stands at the center of the world as the symbol for the process of enlightenment and transformation.

This tree, wide as the heavens itself, has grown up into the heaven from earth. It is an immortal growth and towers between heaven and earth. It is the fulcrum of all things and the place where they are all at rest. It is the foundation of the round world, the center of the cosmos. In it all the diversities in our human nature are formed into a unity. It is held together by the invisible nails of the spirit so that it may not break loose from the divine. It touches the highest summits of heaven and makes the earth firm beneath its foot, and it grasps the middle regions between them with immeasurable arms.

Hyppolytes, Bishop of Rome

The serpent climbs the world tree, which sits between the sun and the moon. It symbolizes the center of the world.

The image of the world represents completion. In your role as the hero, you have now completed your quest. You have undergone the sacred journey of the soul through the cycle of life. Now, for the moment, you are taken out of the cycle, and from this perspective you can glimpse your true self. For a brief instant the psyche is free of the literal, material, self-centered world. For this moment you can be at one with the cosmos and at peace with yourself.

Step VIII in Review

In Step VIII you have reached the point of transformation, the culmination of your pilgrimage past your fears and limitations, to self-realization. Today you are whole and in harmony with all of life. Write down a brief summary of your transformation.

Write down a synthesis of the most important feelings and insights you have gained from your journey along your path.

*The hero has completed his quest, and is taken out of the cycle of life
for a brief moment to glimpse his true self, his inherent divinity.*

Congratulations, You Have Arrived!

Your path has taken you from birth and initiation, into the mysteries within yourself, using symbols to reveal inner truths. You have had a glimpse of the workings underneath, where there is power and wisdom. You have undertaken the quest for your true self, through adversity and through the blackest night of the Devil.

You have survived the assault of your deadliest demons, and they have been tamed. You have come through the journey a stronger and wiser person, more in balance with the inward and outward forces that make you who you are. Thus, your journey has taken you past the Tower and through the forest, along the river and into the ocean of your mind, where all of your questions begin and all of your answers await discovery.

Take a moment to look at your life from this calm and detached perspective; quiet your mind and savor this glimpse of self-knowledge. For this instant you know who you are; you are truly alive and in harmony with yourself.

Capture this moment of vision; find an image that represents this sense of self-understanding to keep with you.

Each time you make this pilgrimage into the deep cosmic waters of the psyche to confront your demons, you will be able to go farther, as you reach for divine inspiration. Remember that your true path lies at the center, where the polarities find balance and the union of the opposites creates a wholeness. It is within this balance that you will find wisdom and understanding to guide you on your journey through life.

Color Index

The colors you pick to represent particular symbols are another way of indicating how you feel about those symbols, and in this way they can give you added information about yourself. If you are very visual and color is an important medium for you, you may want to use felt-tipped pens or colored pencils to fill in the pictures of the Tarot cards at the beginnings of each chapter. In addition, you might want to color any image that seems to be particularly important to you. Then you can look up the meaning of the colors you choose to find out more about your feelings.

God as light is often considered to be the source of color. Warm colors, such as orange, yellow, and red, give back light. Cool colors, such as blue and violet, absorb the light. Green is the synthesis of the two sides of the color chart.

Black—Darkness, chaos, evil, death, despair, destruction, the descent into hell, and thus, as the absence of color, the first stage of rebirth.

Blue—Truth, intellect, wisdom, loyalty, fidelity, prudence, piety, peace, clarity, and intuition. Sky blue is the color of the Great Mother and of the Virgin Mary.

Brown—Renunciation, penitence, and the earth.

Gold—The power of the divine, the sun, enlightenment, immortality, God as light, glory, and radiance.

Green—Made of blue and yellow, green symbolizes heaven and earth, hope and renewal of life, resurrection, gladness, confidence, abundance, growth, fertility, prosperity, and peace. Later, the color green will turn into gold, as in alchemy, the symbol of the ripened corn turns from green to gold. Green is the color of the two lovers. Green is also the color of adaptability and sympathy.

Grey—Humility and penitence, the color of mourning and depression. Grey is also the color of the death of the body and the immortality of the soul. It represents inertia, indifference, and neutralization.

Orange—Luxury, pride, egoism, ambition, and energy. Orange is associated with flames and fire.

Purple—Royalty, power, pride, truth, justice, and temperance. Purple is the color of majestic sovereignty and spirituality.

Red—The sun and war gods, the masculine active principle, fire, royalty, passion, and strength. Red is also the color of anger, vengeance, and death. Depending on the context, it may also represent birth, the mother, and blood.

Silver—The moon, the feminine principle, and virginity.

Violet—Intelligence, knowledge, memory, and nostalgia. It may be associated with grief, mourning old age, and sadness. Violet is also the color of religious devotion and spirituality, sanctity, humility, penitence, and temperance.

White—Perfection, transcendence, light, sun, illumination, purity, chastity, innocence, the sacred. White represents both life and death in that it symbolizes the death of the old and the birth of the new.

Yellow—Light yellow represents intuition, faith, and goodness. Dark yellow is treachery, jealousy, and betrayal.

References

1. Mircea Eliade, *Myths, Dreams and Mysteries* (New York: Harper and Row, 1957), p. 244.

2. Ibid.

3. Ibid., pp. 89–90.

4. Joseph Campbell, *The Hero with a Thousand Faces* (Princeton, N.J.: Princeton/Bollingen, 1973), p. 3.

5. Pierre Grimal, ed. *Larousse World Mythology* (Secaucus, N.J.: Chartwell Books, 1965), p. 10.

6. Adapted from Donald Attwater's *The Penguin Dictionary of Saints* (Baltimore: Penguin Books, 1965), p. 201.

7. A. Vasiliev, *The History of the Byzantine Empire*, Vol. 2 (Madison and Milwaukee: University of Wisconsin Press, 1964), p. 653.

8. Hans Jonas, *The Gnostic Religion* (Boston: Beacon Press, 1958), pp. 89–90.

9. Eliade, *Myths, Dreams and Mysteries*, p. 183.

10. Ibid., p. 184.

11. Campbell, *The Hero with a Thousand Faces*, p. 11.

12. Dante, *The Divine Comedy*.

13. Mircea Eliade, *Patterns in Comparative Religion* (Cleveland: World Publishing Co., 1958), p. 154.

14. Dante, *The Divine Comedy*.

15. Eliade, *Myths, Dreams and Mysteries*, p. 82.

16. A. Guilaumont et al., *The Gospel According to Thomas* (New York: Harper and Brothers, 1959), p. vi.

17. Dante, *The Divine Comedy*.

Bibliography

Benson, Herbert, M. D. *The Relaxation Response.* Avon Books, New York, 1975.

Boas, Franz. *Race, Language and Culture.* Free Press, New York, 1940.

Brown, Barbara. *New Mind, New Body.* Bantam Books, New York, 1974.

Butler, W. E. *Magic and the Qabalah.* Aquarian Press, London, 1964.

Cade, C. Maxwell, and Nona Coxhead. *The Awakened Mind.* Delta Books, Dell Publishing, New York, 1974.

Campbell, Joseph. *The Flight of the Wild Gander: Explorations in the Mythological Dimension.* Viking, New York, 1969.

_____. *The Hero with a Thousand Faces.* Bollingen Series XVII, Princeton University Press, Princeton, N.J., 1973.

_____. *The Masks of God.* 4 vols. Viking Compass Books, New York, 1970.

_____. *Myths to Live By.* Bantam Books, New York, 1972.

Dante, *The Divine Comedy.* Lawrence White, trans. Parthenon Books, New York, 1978.

De Laurence, L. W. *The Illustrated Key to the Tarot.* De Laurence, Scott and Company, Chicago, 1918.

de Sousa, Herbert A., *Six Simple Steps to Meditation.* Loyola University, Los Angeles, 1979.

Doane, Doris Chase, and King Keys. *Tarot Card Spread Reader.* Parker Publishing, West Nyack, N.Y., 1967.

Edinger, Edward. *Ego and Archetype.* Pelican Books, Baltimore, 1972.

Eliade, Mircea. *Myths, Dreams and Mysteries.* Harper and Row, New York, 1957.

_____. *Patterns in Comparative Religion.* Meridian Books, World Publishing, Cleveland, 1968.

_____. *The Myth of the Eternal Return.* W. R. Trask, trans. Pantheon, New York, 1954.

Fabry, Joseph. *The Pursuit of Meaning.* Harper and Row, New York, 1968.

Ferguson, Marilyn. *The Aquarian Conspiracy*. Jeremy P. Tarcher, Los Angeles, 1980.

Gray, Eden. *A Complete Guide to the Tarot*. Bantam Books, New York, 1970.

Greer, Mary K. *Tarot for Your Self*. Newcastle Publishing, North Hollywood, Calif., 1984.

Harding, Esther. *Psychic Energy*. Bollingen Series X, Princeton University Press, Princeton, N.J., 1973.

Hillman, James. *Re-Visioning Psychology*. Harper and Row, New York, 1977.

Houston, Jean. *The Possible Human*. Jeremy P. Tarcher, Los Angeles, 1982.

Jonas, Hans. *The Gnostic Religion*. Beacon Press, Boston, 1958.

Jung, C. G. (with C. Kereyni). *Essays on a Science of Mythology*. Bollingen Series XXII, Princeton University Press, Princeton, N.J., 1973.

_____. *Psyche and Symbol*. Doubleday and Company, Garden City, N.Y., 1958.

_____. *Psychology and Alchemy*. R. F. C. Hull, trans. Bollingen Foundation, New York, 1953.

_____. *The Undiscovered Self*. Mentor Books, New York, 1957.

Kereyni, C. *The Gods of the Greeks*. Thames and Hudson, London, 1951.

Newman, Erich. *The Great Mother*. Bollingen Series XLII, Princeton University Press, Princeton, N.J., 1972.

Nichols, Sallie. *Jung and the Tarot: An Archetypal Journey*. Samuel Weiser, New York, 1980.

Pearce, Joseph Chilton. *Exploring the Crack in the Cosmic Egg*. Simon and Schuster, New York, 1975.

Peck, M. Scott. *The Road Less Traveled*. Touchstone Books, New York, 1978.

Progoff, Ira. *Depth Psychology and Modern Man*. McGraw-Hill Paperbacks, New York, 1969.

_____. *Jung, Synchronicity and Human Destiny: Noncausal Dimensions of Human Experience*. Dell/Delta, New York, 1973.

_____. *The Symbolic and the Real*. McGraw-Hill Paperbacks, New York, 1973.

Rank, Otto. *The Myth of the Birth of the Hero and Other Writings*. Philip Freund, ed. Vintage Books, New York, 1959.

Samuels, Mike, and Hal Bennett. *Spirit Guides: Access to Inner Worlds.* Random House/Bookworks, New York, Berkeley, 1974.

Schaya, Leo. *The University Meaning of the Kabbalah.* Penguin Books, Baltimore, 1974.

Schnur, Harry C., ed. Apuleius, *The Golden Ass.* Crowell-Collier Publishing Co., New York, 1962.

Scholem, Gershom, ed. Zohar, *The Book of Splendor.* Schocken Books, New York, 1966.

Tart, Charles T., ed. *Altered States of Consciousness.* Doubleday Anchor Books, Garden City, N.Y., 1969.

Underhill, Evelyn. *Mysticism: A Study in the Nature and Development of Man's Spiritual Consciousness.* Methuen & Company, London, 1949.

von Franz, Marie-Louise. *Alchemy.* Inner City Books, Toronto, 1980.

Waite, A. E. *The Holy Kabbalah.* University Books, New Hyde Park, N.Y., 1965.

Watts, Alan W. *Psychotherapy East and West.* Pantheon Books, New York, 1969.